# YOU GOTTA KEEP DANCIN'

May God
Bless,
Suzie

Giver of life, creator of all that is lovely,
  Teach me to sing the words to your song;
I want to feel the music of living
  And not fear the sad songs
But from them make new songs
  Composed of both laughter and tears.

Teach me to dance to the sounds of your world
              and your people,
  I want to move in rhythm with your plan,
Help me to try to follow your leading
  To risk even falling
  To rise and keep trying
Because you are leading the dance.

AUTHOR UNKNOWN

TIM HANSEL

# YOU GOTTA KEEP DANCIN'

David C. Cook Publishing Co.

David C. Cook Publishing Co., Elgin, Illinois 60120
David C. Cook Publishing Co., Weston, Ontario

YOU GOTTA KEEP DANCIN'
© 1985 by Tim Hansel.

Cover design by Chris Patchel
Scripture references, unless otherwise noted, are from the New
International Version

First printing, 1985
Printed in the United States of America
90 89 88 87    10 9 8 7 6


Library of Congress Cataloging in Publication Data

Hansel, Tim.
    You gotta keep dancin'.

    1. Hansel, Tim. 2. Christian biography—United States. 3. Suf-
fering—Religious aspects—Christianity. I. Title.
BR1725.H235A36 1985 248.8'6'0924 [B] 85-11298
ISBN 0-89191-722-5

*To Pam*
*who shared my struggle*
*throughout the entire journey,*
*and loved me anyway.*

*To the Lows*
*Gary, Peg, Susan, and Peggy*
*who gave me reason for hope, and*
*even celebration, in spite of it all.*
*Thanks for believing in me and*
*encouraging me enough to make this*
*book a reality.*

# Contents

# God's
# Unknown Verbs

This book was inspired by some of God's unknown heroes—those verbs and exclamation points that we pass every day without recognizing the living vibrant texture of Christ within them. Their lives contain so much beauty, so much growth, and so much change—but it is often hidden in pain or awkwardness. These are everyday heroes who have chosen not to be victims but gallant fighters in spite of incredible odds. For them, and because of them, this book was written.

The constellation of lives which inspired and illuminate these pages are real. Their pain is not theoretical, their struggles are not sophisticated, their heartache is all too tangible, but their hope and tenacity are incorrigible. They have, without knowing it, revealed to me a living Christ who transcends *all* difficulties and circumstances. They have quietly and joyfully shared his life by sharing theirs so freely. Their courage, their faith, their laughter, and their tears have taught me a whole new alphabet of grace and given new meaning to words like dignity and freedom.

My special thanks to all my "Go for It" friends ("Go

for It" is a special Summit Expedition wilderness course for the physically disabled). To Leigh, who taught me tenacity. To Runner, who taught me incorrigible joy. To Bob, who taught me without eyes of his own how to see. To Tre, who taught me the meaning of wholeness and health. To Joyce, who taught me compassion. To Zane, who taught me commitment. To Tim, who taught me hope and the real meaning of the words, "Oh, wow!" To Dave, who is still teaching me what it means to glorify God with our bodies. And Mark, who is helping me to realize that in the end we can't lose. To Matt, who has redefined the word giant for me. To Mike and Carol, who have helped me know the true meaning of words like courage and joy, and to Julie, whose smile is wonderfully contagious. There have been many like Ruth and Georgie, Jim and Rick, Craig and John, "Coop" and Dennis, Wes and Howard, and Gaff and Hans, who have "kept me dancin' " when I wanted to quit. Thanks, Ty, for your indomitable enthusiasm. And a very special thanks to Erma and Steve, who hung in there with me in spite of some difficult times of transition. "Sven Torn," as we are fond of calling him, is a living example of what this book is all about.

To Jack and Peb and Charlie and Paul, for faithful friendship far beyond the call. And to Jerry Hay and Summit Expedition's new board, who came in amidst broken dreams and helped us put it all back together again. To Dr. Willie Martinez, who put my life back together after the fall, and to Dr. George Halburian, who has given more than just his matchless skill to keep me going.

To Bev O'Gorman Thorn, Sherry Billups, and Esther Bullock, who have spent countless hours putting these words end to end on paper in spite of their own demanding schedules, so that these stories could be shared. Finally, to Cathy Davis and LoraBeth Norton, whose affirmation and uncanny editorial skills made this book possible.

# Because God Loves Stories

*Life can be counted on*
*to provide*
*all the pain*
*that any of us might need.*

SHELDON KOPP

I can't remember when I last woke up feeling good.
Each morning continues another layer of nauseating
pain, stiffness, the dull gray ache, and the never-ending
fatigue. It's been a little over ten years since my
accident. Life was different before then; I just can't
remember what it felt like.

PAIN. It seems to be the common denominator of
our human existence. It's part of the life experience. To
avoid it is to detour the essence of life itself.

My publishers have been after me for some time to
write about this journey, but I've been very reluctant. I
know full well that I'm still in the midst of the
pilgrimage, and I suppose I always will be. I felt that I
needed to bring the process to completion in my own

life before I could begin to share with others what I have learned. But, as an old Chinese proverb says, "Were I to await perfection, my book would never be finished."

This is a book about life. Real life. It will probably be the most difficult book I will ever write, and the most personal. There is a delicate balance between being honest and being overly dramatic. I want to admit struggle without giving way to despair. And I want the ultimate message to be positive without sounding pious or tinny.

The pain in my personal journey has been all too real, but so has the joy. This book is in no way meant to diminish the awfulness of pain, tragedy, and affliction. I don't want to "celebrate pain," but more deeply understand the dignity of what can happen in it, through it, and because of it.

I want this book to offer some hope to those who suffer, for whatever reason, but I don't intend it as "advice." It's hard to be self-righteous when you have been broken, at times almost completely, by the process.

Over twenty years ago, I was given a poem that I've carried with me ever since. Somehow it seems appropriate at the beginning of this book.

## Sharing

There isn't much that I can do, but I can share my bread with you, and sometimes share a sorrow, too—as on our way we go.

There isn't much that I can do, but I can sit an hour with you, and I can share a joke with you, and sometimes share reverses, too—as on our way we go.

There isn't much that I can do, but I can share my flowers with you, and I can share my books with you

and sometimes share your burdens, too—as on our way
we go.

There isn't much that I can do, but I can share my
songs with you, and I can share my mirth with you, and
sometimes come and laugh with you—as on our way we
go.

There isn't much that I can do, but I can share my
hopes with you, and I can share my fears with you, and
sometimes shed some tears with you—as on our way we
go.

There isn't much that I can do, but I can share my
friends with you, and I can share my life with you, and
oftentimes share a prayer with you—as on our way we
go.

AUTHOR UNKNOWN

Each human season, each life happening, serves to
sharpen the possibilities and underline the uniqueness
of each life. There are no "typical stories," as there are
no typical lives. When it comes to living, there is no such
thing as ordinary. As Elie Wiesel said, "God made man
because he loves stories."

*This is one of them.*

# PART ONE

# A BLESSED RAGE TO LIVE

*My assumption is that the story of any one of us is in some measure the story of us all.*

Frederick Buechner

# An Eternal Moment in Time

*Give me silence, water, hope*
*give me struggle, iron, volcanoes*
                               EDWARD ABBEY

*O God . . . lead me to the rock that is higher than I.*
                                     PSALM 61:1, 2

FOUR-THIRTY A.M. CONCENTRATED STILLNESS. The moisture from our breath hangs like icicles from the inside of our small mountain tent. Lying only an inch above the snow, yet snugly warm inside our down bags, the vivid contrast underlines the wonder of being alive. Crisp, clear coldness and silence so thick that the sound of the small stove hums like a twelve-foot bumblebee.

Outside a black-and-white world. The Palisade Glacier, hundreds of feet thick, as indelible as the darkness that holds it in place. In a breath of time the miracle of every day will happen again. The sun will rise. But this time we will see it. The miracle of light and life reborn.

Sun. Son. Rise. Again. In me. This morning.

Three men in a tent. Crowded but uncluttered.

21

Pushing back the blurry cobwebs of sleep, but excited. Weary from the long hike in, but eager. Moving with deliberateness, but not hurry. Hurry forgets, makes mistakes. In situations like this, mistakes can be fatal.

Why we came no longer matters: what happened changed my life forever. Breakfast is brief: cold cereal and hot cocoa with instant coffee in it—"super cocoa." We check our gear. Twice. Three times. Ropes. Biners. Ice screws. Ice axes. Webbing. It will be a mixed climb, so we need rock climbing gear as well. Slings. Hexes. Stoppers. More carabiners. The trick is to find that perfect balance between lightness and completeness. Too much weight is dangerous, likewise too little equipment.

*More of life should be like this,* I think. We've become so insulated. A person can go a whole lifetime in our society without getting really cold, really hot, really tired, really thirsty. Too much padding, too little life at this essential level. Living on the edge always has its own rewards. Fullness. Richness. All the senses alive!

The sun is almost up. We've got to get moving. We want to be on the couloir, across the big crevasse at the bottom, before the sun. The firmer the ice the faster we climb. And the safer.

Only two of us will climb today. Roger will wait at base camp and enjoy the solitude, watch the earth turn from this most splendid vantage point. As a high school teacher, he enjoys being out in this original classroom where bells don't ring every fifty minutes. Time to remember, to think, to become whole again. He'll be able to watch much of the climb from a distance.

Camping on the glacier was a good idea. Within thirty minutes we are at the crevasse. Conveniently for us, a snow bridge crosses it.

The climb will consist of four to five pitches (lengths of rope), or about 800 feet of snow and ice and then four pitches of rock climbing. Already we anticipate having lunch at over 14,000 feet, with a view of almost a hundred miles. The Sierras are as magnificent as any range in the world, and as varied.

Young, strong, experienced, David is a superb partner. He leads the first pitch, as I think to myself, this has got to be the most beautiful place on earth. There are many such places; we just don't make the effort to find them.

I'm glad to be moving. Our incredible internal combustion systems have a way of turning a simple breakfast into warmth, energy, and even joy! This morning I feel especially glad to be alive.

We alternate leads. I'm impressed with how gracefully and smoothly David climbs. My style is more akin to a rhinoceros on snowshoes, earning me the nickname "Thrasher" among the Summit staff. But what I lack in finesse, I usually try to make up for in perseverance. I have a habit of tenaciously getting to the top. Like Mutt and Jeff, we alternate leads to the top of the couloir.

I've always liked rock better than snow and ice, so I feel somewhat relieved to reach the base of the dihedral. Snow and ice have beauty and grace, but rock affords a sense of security and stability. The first pitch is fairly straightforward. It feels good to be using all of my body and all of my mind. Climbing not only allows it, but demands it.

> Our bodies are shot with mortality (and immortality). · Our legs are fear and our arms are time. . . . That is why physical courage is so important—it fills, as it were, the holes. . . .[1]
>
> ANNIE DILLARD

So we fill the holes with rock-climbing gear and courage and laughter and encouragement. Like spiders on a nylon web of time, we cling to the rock and to each other.

"Our life is a faint tracing on the surface of the mystery," says Annie Dillard. We experience it as fully as we know how and share our "choir of proper praise" on top. What an extravagant gesture of the Creator are the Sierras! It's as if we can see the whole show of creation. I know many who pay enormous amounts of money to dine somewhere with a view, but we have lunch in a place that money can't buy. A view worth the time, risk, and effort.

All moments in time are just that—moments—so they must, by definition, come to an end. Stiff and satisfied by the exertion, we pack up the lunch remains and unpack the necessary gear for the descent. We will do a series of rappels down to the interface between the ice and rock, and then belay each other while down-climbing to the base of the couloir.

Snow has many personalities. In the period of a day, it changes constantly. We're aware that, affected by shade and sunlight and time, the snow is different going down than coming up. At the bottom I let out a "Hot dang!" of glee. We congratulate each other on a job well done. From here all we have to do is cross the snow bridge and head back to our base camp. We can see the tent in the distance. We feel secure in crampons, standing eight to ten feet above the crevasse. At that angle it is no more difficult than standing on a roof.

I wonder if a lot of accidents happen in the late afternoon. Weary, satisfied from the day's fullness, maybe we're especially prone to errors in thinking. Ordinarily it doesn't pose a problem, but up here minor errors can have major consequences. Mountaineering, like life, has far more subtleties than we twentieth-century moviegoers sometimes realize.

The snow had changed. At that particular time of day it has some unique characteristics which may only last for twenty to thirty minutes. Little details. Unbeknown to the climber, snow can ball up under his crampons, packing the spikes full, leaving only the tips exposed. Then the simple walk on the roof becomes more like skating.

But still, it's not a major problem. Should he fall, any experienced climber can do a self-arrest with his ice ax, which stops him immediately. Usually. But the snow had changed at that particular moment in time. At that particular place the consistency was just soft enough, just heavy enough, to make it more difficult. Difficult enough that if one should slip, if he were to do a self-arrest, if he needed to stop, he could—but it would take a little longer. Maybe even one moment too long.

David was halfway across the bridge when my crampons balled up. I slipped. Just as I was beginning to stop, my feet went over the edge. The momentum gave gravity just enough of a nudge to cause me to flip upside down. Little details.

I don't remember what I was thinking—probably nothing. Certainly nothing profound. I still didn't believe it was happening, but David did. Sometimes I think I still feel worse for him than for me—having to stand helplessly watching the whole event, unable to assist.

As he described it to me later, "The whole thing seemed to be in slow motion. You flipped over and floated, upside down, toward the bottom. It was like some old Spencer Tracy movie where someone fell and took forever to land. It took so long for you to hit."

But eventually I did, landing on the ice at the bottom. It could have been worse. I still had a short ice ax wrapped around my wrist, and why I wasn't skewered on it like a barbecue was a blessing—maybe a miracle. And the large domed rock at the bottom could easily have broken my neck. Instead, when I finally came to, my arm was draped around a large angular stone, the way a guy holds a girl on his first high school date. The ice ax lay, still wrapped on my wrist, on the other side.

But it could have been better, too. Had I not flipped over, I would have crunched my legs instead of my upper body. Had there been something other than air to break my fall, the impact might not have been so devastating. At thirty-two feet per second, I arrived rather quickly. Since then I've quipped that the fall didn't bother me at all, but the landing on the bottom made something of an impact on my body.

When I came to, David was kneeling beside me, asking me questions. We were both glad I opened my eyes. To his surprise, and my own, I sat up. After a lengthy pause in that position, I stood. A little wobbly, but vertical. The thing I remember the most was feeling very short, as though my six-foot-two frame had been compacted into a new two-foot-nine design. I joyfully tested movement in all my limbs. Positive. But I still felt short.

I also felt lucky. Very lucky. I always knew that I had an angel on my shoulder—he had simply been working overtime again. David and I came to the joyful conclusion that I'd had a bad fall with a miracle ending. Not only did my limbs still move, but we still made the toughest climb of the day getting out.

Back on the glacier we even talked of more climbs,

but we knew that this was enough for one day. At base camp, we filled Roger in on all the details. The climb was glorious. And we were very lucky.

I still felt short. I thought I could walk in and out of our tiny tent without bending over—and bending over was difficult. By now I was very sore. I felt as though I had a migraine headache all over my body. David had some strong medication in the first-aid kit. It dulled the pain only slightly, but enough that I could sleep. We had to get some rest, as there was still an eight-hour hike out the next day.

I still had a headache in the morning and I felt as though I only came up to my belt. I said, "I'd fix breakfast, but I don't think I can reach the handle on the stove."

I don't remember much of the hike out. Everyone has headaches, I thought. No big deal. And it's okay to be short. A lot of great people are short. But I still kept pulling up on my chin in the hopes that I could get my ears off my boot tops.

We had dinner together. I don't remember what I ate. We all talked about what a great climb it was and how lucky I had been. We agreed that it had been a close call. "We'd have hated to have to carry you out of there," the others said. "Our packs were enough."

They headed north. A long drive, trading off, would get David and Roger home after midnight. I headed south alone.

I'm sure lucky, I thought. And weary. I'll get some coffee at the next town.

I'm still weary. I've got gear; maybe I'll just camp overnight alongside the road. The eastern side of the Sierras has miles of desert. I phoned Pam.

"No problem," she said. "How was the climb?"

"Great! How's Zac?" My first child—a boy. I hoped he would love adventure, too. "I'll see you sometime after lunch, babe. Give ol' Zac a hug for me."

Man, I'm tired. I'm going to find a camping spot as soon as I can. I hope I can reach the steering wheel. Wish I weren't so darn short.

I don't remember sleeping much. Sunrise comes early in the desert. I'll stop somewhere for breakfast instead of fixing it here. Yeah, that's a good idea.

I don't remember much of the drive home. I was just glad to get there.

David and I had agreed that we wouldn't mention anything about the fall to Pam. It would only scare her. I'd had lots of bumps and bruises from football and nine years of rugby. This was just one more in a long string of puzzles for my body to solve.

My love for Pam and for my newborn son did much to relieve the pain. So much that I no longer cared that I was shorter, and Pam didn't even notice. In fact, she would never have known that I'd had a little spill on the mountain, had I not woken up the next night sweating profusely, delirious, in incredible pain, and not knowing where I was. I was coming out of shock.

The body. What an amazing mechanism. I never would have made it home had it not been for my body's incredible ability to rise to the occasion. But now it was beginning to come apart at the seams.

Pam asked the obvious.

"Oh, it was only a little fall. I'm fortunate, babe. I really am."

\*     \*     \*

"We'd better phone a doctor."
"Okay."

\* \* \*

X rays. I wonder how many hundreds, thousands of times I've been x-rayed. They've seen everything there is to see.

"What do you see, Doc?"

\* \* \*

"Can you turn your head? Raise your arms if you can."

\* \* \*

The beginning of an incredible journey.

# A Blessed Rage
# to Live

*Be merciful to me, Lord, for I am faint;*
  *O Lord, heal me, for my bones are in agony.*
*My soul is in anguish.*
  *How long, O Lord, how long?*

PSALM 6:2, 3

*You purchase pain with all that joy can give*
*and die of nothing but a rage to live.*

ALEXANDER POPE

*He who has this disease called Jesus will never be cured.*

OLD RUSSIAN PROVERB

SHARING PERSONAL JOURNALS is a bit like opening one's underwear drawer in public. You're not quite sure what you will find, and there is a strong chance that you will be embarrassed. My journal keeping was never done with the thought that it would be shared with others. It was simply my attempt at catharsis and clarity as I sought to find a pattern amidst the pain and confusion.

But as these words from Tolstoy suggest, there is value in honest sharing: "A writer is dear and necessary for us only in the measure of which he reveals to us the innerworkings of his very soul." Or from Nietzsche, "Of all that is written, I love only what a person has written with his own blood."

*       *       *

*Fall, 1974*
*Bad news. Like Jacob, I've wrestled with God, and lost—and may be lame for the rest of my life. It looks like I may have to hold on to him long enough for him to bless me, too. X-rays from the fall show fractures in the vertebrae, crushed discs, and some fragments of bone in my neck. The doctor said he was not surprised that now that the shock was wearing off that I would be experiencing some rather intense pain. He called that one right. I suppose, in the long run, I'm just grateful to be alive. As I look back on it, I'm very fortunate to still be around—and can't believe I'm still able to move all my limbs. It all depends on how you look at it—perhaps I'm blessed beyond measure just to still be here.*

*I feel almost dismembered this morning by outrageous pain. It is almost comical to have reached such a ludicrous level of disorder. Me, with my desire to be agile and free, barely able to get up and out of a chair this morning. Teach me to live in new ways, O Lord. Teach me and show me your ways in the midst of this.*

*In times like these of such intense physical pain, confusion and doubt, one must simply decide and do, decide and do—and laugh a bit amidst the consequences.*

*       *       *

According to the doctors, the damage was done and my situation was relatively stable. In other words, my "only problem" would be pain, so they allowed me to go home. I didn't realize how terribly difficult it would be to maintain perspective. Although I "played with pain" when I played football and rugby at Stanford, this was quantitatively and qualitatively different. I never knew that just getting around the house could be so difficult—just the walk from the bedroom to the bathroom seemed impossible. Though no stranger to pain, I was learning some new rules—and boundaries.

\* \* \*

*Fall, 1974*
*This is a time of great fatigue and disorientation. If I only knew how long it was going to last. "What I want from you is your true thanks. I want you to trust me in your times of trouble so that I can rescue you and you can give me joy."*

*I realize that for days I have been so self-preoccupied that I have closed out all the windows of light. Help me to will your will, Lord. Help me to get outside of my own puny preoccupations.*

*Zachary, which means "he whom God remembers," celebrated his first Thanksgiving today by walking. He still looks a little like a midget wino, wobbling from chair to chair, but his tiny life reminds us of the many little things and big that we are thankful for today.*

*Winter, 1974*
*My wife—what a woman! Steeped in patience, molded in love. I shall never understand why I'm so fortunate as to have a life companion such as this. Sometimes I think this process is more difficult for her than it is on me.*

*Spring, 1975*
*The doctor said today to begin to learn to live with intense
pain, because it would probably be around for a lifetime. The
diagnosis is that the fractures and crushed discs, on impact of
the fall, have caused traumatic deteriorating arthritis. I asked
him why he kept emphasizing the word "deteriorating." To
which he replied, "I'm only being honest—that's what's really
going to happen." He also indicated that there is massive soft
tissue damage, which I don't fully comprehend. He says that the
ligaments, tendons, and muscles have also been damaged,
perhaps beyond repair. I was to be congratulated for having
done such a fine job of rearranging my personal body
structure. According to the news, I had just missed becoming a
robot.*

*I feel like I'm in a walking coma. Coherence eludes me.
Sometimes it's almost frightening to close my eyes and sleep, for
fear that I might not wake up. Oftentimes during the day, I
have real difficulty staying conscious. I know neither what is
wrong with me nor what is keeping me going. However, if
these symptoms continue, I will probably ask to be hospitalized
again. I'm sure that the strain on Pam is becoming almost
unbearable. I have tried with all my limited endurance to show
no signs of my discomfort for the past many months, but I think
my disguise has worn thin.*

*Tonight—another night of not being able to sleep for the pain
and symptoms—it's all moving to proportions that I can no
longer handle.*

\*     \*     \*

Pain. We all know what it tastes like. Whether its
source is physical, emotional, mental, or spiritual, its

interruption in our lives disrupts and reshapes. It intercepts our hopes and plans; it rearranges our dreams. It always leaves a mark.

I realized again each day that *all* of our lives are terminal. Only time and quality differ. The choice for all of us is not *if* we will accept pain, but *how.*

I chose to accept the pain as aggressively as possible. I continued my work with Summit Expedition, a wilderness/mountaineering ministry which Pam and I had started in 1970. I kept on climbing, jogging, and playing tennis—until the day I discovered that my spine wasn't quite as stable as the doctors had thought.

Playing tennis with a friend, I was delivering my strongest serve when there was a loud crack. Jim thought I had broken my racket. What had actually happened was that I had torn several ribs from my spine (but I aced the serve). After a week spent in traction, I came home wearing a body cast from my belt up . . . and the pain had made a quantitative and qualitative leap.

My emotions were like a Duncan yo-yo. I discovered real depression firsthand. I had no idea how to antici- pate the pain or cope with it. Perhaps I was going through the stages identified by Kubler-Ross in relation to death and dying. These stages apply to any kind of loss, that of a loved one or of a part of oneself.

The first stage is *denial*—not believing that it's really happening. The second stage is *bargaining*, trying to equivocate with God to make deals. The third stage is *anger*, the rage that comes from within based upon frustration which cannot be satiated. The fourth stage is *depression*, a symptom of both prolonged anger turned inward and guilt. The final stage is *acceptance*, realizing that what is, is—and is going to be.

Still a long way from genuine acceptance, I was struggling in my own limited way to make sense of all that was going on. By now the doctors had put me on Percodan, one of the strongest oral narcotics a person can take.

I got a friend to saw a split in the cast so I could slip out of it occasionally, and the medication numbed me enough that I attempted to keep on working. Friends and staff were gracious and tolerant, to say the least. All too often, their patience and Pam's was stretched far beyond human limits. So was my endurance. In fact, there were times when I wasn't sure how much I wanted to go on living.

*       *       *

*Summer, 1975*
*I go into the hospital Monday morning again for more tests and such.*
*Despair.*
*So real.*
*So deep.*

*Paralyzed in my own pain, cynicism, and ugliness. I feel so inept, so weak, so ugly, that I want to shun even myself. I don't want to be around anyone when I'm this way, and yet I'm sure I can't solve this by myself. Everything seems like such a hassle. On days like this I feel that I've wasted most of my life.*

*More X rays. More bad news. I've realized more strongly than ever that you don't truly discover your roots until you are at the bottom of the pit. From this perspective you are no longer distracted by usual superficialities which disguise themselves in masks of importance. I looked up the word "root." It means "to dig down in some mass in order to find something valuable."*

*In higher orders of living things, a means of support, a reservoir of life energy. The cause, the source, the essence, the essential points or parts. The music root refers to that tone from which all other harmonies, overtones, and chords are produced. In philosophy, it is the uncompounded and uncompromised word or element without prefix, suffix, or inflectional ending. And, finally, it means "to be or become firmly established, to plant or fix deeply," as in the earth. God is teaching me through all this to rediscover the substance of my strength and my song. Perhaps this is an unusual opportunity to discover who I really am.*

\*　　\*　　\*

I had a choice. I knew by now that the damage was permanent, and that pain would be a companion for the rest of my journey. I had to learn a whole new way of living or fold up my cards. The deck was stacked. The life I'd always known was never to be again.

Slowly my rage to live emerged from the depression, frustration, and anger. But when it was there I realized that it had a taste to it that I'd never known before. I began to see life in a way that never would have been possible before. I began to relish small, daily, simple things—and realized at a depth that never seemed possible that *all* of life was sacred. There were moments, though sporadic and far apart, when I began to understand that life wasn't over for me—but perhaps was just beginning.

\*　　\*　　\*

*Fall, 1975*
*If you can't change circumstances, change the way you respond to them.*

*It has been said that there is no such thing as a problem that doesn't have a gift in it. I'm going to have to begin to find some of those gifts and open them.*

*Even in the midst of all this, there is no better time than the now. Open your eyes—otherwise the beauty will pass you by. Open your heart—else the truth will not walk with you.*

*Winter, 1975*
*It does appear as though I'm learning Grace the hard way. But I am slowly learning—and for what I've discovered the price may be worth it. Good education, but the tuition is high.*

*Each morning, new hope. Life is more difficult, and at times strangely more delicious than it's ever been. I will continue to* choose *to make it so.*

*Perhaps this is the ultimate realization—when we recognize that all the questions have the same answer that comes from you, O Lord, from you.*

\*     \*     \*

I'm not sure which was hardest to deal with—the pain or the doubt, the frustration or the fear. All life's questions seemed to be intensified. The disillusionment with our own abilities is, perhaps, one of the most important things that can ever happen to us. But the process can be terrifying.

I was being stretched in so many different directions at once—struggling to surrender and fully accept what was inevitable, and yet wanting to know where and how to fight it all as well. There seemed to be a fine line between giving up and giving in.

\*     \*     \*

*Spring, 1976*
*There seems to be no refuge from the pain and fatigue. "Man*
*was born to live, to suffer, and to die—and whatever befalls*
*him is a tragic lot. There is no denying this in the final end, but*
*we must . . . deny it all the way" (Thomas Wolfe). I don't*
*understand, Lord, either what or why or where you are taking*
*me. But grant me the strength to either surrender or defy it all.*
*Should it serve your strong purpose, continue to break me.*

*At times I whisper in the night: "God, I've learned enough*
*now! I'm ready for the next test."*

*Summer, 1976*
*You think that fear will go away—but it doesn't.*

*Learning patience . . . takes a lot of patience.*

*What a test of character adversity is. It can either destroy or*
*build up, depending on our chosen response. Pain can either*
*make us better or bitter.*

*It feels like everything is falling down around me—and*
*everything is falling apart within me.*

\*     \*     \*

I knew I had come to a critical place in my life. I had
to choose either to break down or break through.

# Breakdown or Breakthrough

*Argue for your limitations long enough and, sure enough, they're yours.*
                                                    RICHARD BACH

*You must carry the chaos within you in order to give birth to the dancing star.*
                                                    NIETZSCHE

ALL OF OUR THEOLOGY must eventually become biography. The constant challenge in this life we call Christian is the translation of all we believe to be true into our day-to-day life-style.

My accident, I began to realize, was more than just an interruption in my life, more than just a meddlesome interlude. It was a major intersection.

The crossroads forced a choice, but the choice was neither easy nor obvious. At times the best I could do was muddle.

*Fall, 1976*
*My frustration is almost as high as it's ever been, Lord. What*

*does it mean to "surrender" all of these feelings to you?*

*One of the big problems with pain is that it is so myopic. Nothing robs one's strength and vitality so much as self-absorption. There is no greater waste of time than self-pity, preoccupation with self; it fragments and dissipates that which you want to be about. Oh, God, you seem to have the only key that can unlock me from myself.*

*Woke up again in the middle of the night in sickening pain, unable to sleep, struggling to thank him for all this.*

*   *   *

There continued to be days, and nights, where the pain seemed so unceasing that I didn't know what to do. Without knowing it, I was being reduced to the bare essentials of faith.

*   *   *

*Winter, 1976*
*Faith plus nothing equals that which pleases God.*

*Grace is merely letting God find you.*

*Faith isn't really faith until it's all that you're holding on to.*

*Lord, when I want you least, I need you most.*

*God will never lead you where his grace cannot keep you.*

*   *   *

The pain didn't decrease as I (in spite of the doctors' statements) had hoped it would. But I did begin to learn new ways to respond to it.

\*     \*     \*

*Spring, 1977*
*He who laughs . . . lasts.*

*Quite possibly the pain and the nausea give me an advantage in having to concentrate, focus more thoroughly and choose more deliberately, because otherwise my energy dissipates so quickly. Anything, I suppose, has the opportunity of being a privilege.*

*Summer, 1977*
*Humble me, Lord, no matter what the consequences.*

*God, grant me the serenity to remember who I am.*

*Fall, 1977*
*I'm grateful for the painful ways in which God is pruning me for a greater kind of strength and gentleness. Now is the season toward deliberate love which transcends circumstances—and a deliberate gratitude and joy which will be exercised in faith alone.*

*May I decrease—that he may increase.*

*Only empty hands can receive. Pain is only another road to wisdom.*

*Winter, 1977*
*The only thing that is permanent is change. These changes are bringing about some difficult transitions—primarily, how I look at life and how I look at myself. For so long my self-image depended on my physical strength and fitness. Now I'm being forced to far deeper dimensions. Never apologize for being who*

*you are—even now. Never, never, never, never—it is a sin of the first order. No apologies. No excuses. No regrets. No complaints.*

*Pam surprised me this morning when she said, "Your self-respect in the midst of this is what I admire in you the most." And then she continued, "I hope you never give it away by compromise."*

*Spring, 1978*
*If your security is based on something that can be taken away from you—you will constantly be on a false edge of security.*

*Fall, 1978*
*Perhaps this pain has forced some kind of awakening in me. It has established not only a new durability of the spirit and a new endurance of the heart, but also a wild and tenacious vividness of life. It is as though I've been forewarned—therefore, blessed—by the ensuing and insistent pain. Slowly I'm even learning to trust the pain like a friend, to learn from it like a mentor, embrace it like a brother, and laugh at it like a . . . a fool for Christ's sake. My eyes have been opened to see so much more of life than I would have been willing to do so otherwise. A new odyssey awaits me and I am ready.*

\*     \*     \*

Part of the change came from being willing to "lean into the pain," as Clyde Reid explains it in his book, *Celebrate the Temporary:*

> One of the most common obstacles to celebrating life fully is our avoidance of pain. We dread pain. We fear pain. We do anything to escape pain. Our culture reinforces our avoidance of pain by assuring us that we can live a painless life.

44

Advertisements constantly encourage us to believe that life can be pain-free (but) to live without pain is a myth . . . To live without pain . . . is to live half-alive, without fullness of life. This is an unmistakable, clear, unalterable fact. . . . Many of us do not realize that pain and joy run together. When we cut ourselves off from pain, we have unwittingly cut ourselves off from joy as well.[1]

Many people who know of my current deep commitment to joy in spite of the circumstances ask how or when the change occurred. My best answer is, "I don't know." Like most good things in my life, it happened more by grace than by intention.

But in looking back, I can observe a few events that were instrumental. The first contributing factor was that I was asked to write a book. No one was more surprised than I the night Ron Wilson called me and asked if I would write a book on celebrating life. He said he wanted to explore the concepts of leisure, joy, and celebration from a Christian standpoint. Since I was working four jobs in order to keep our Summit Expedition ministry alive, I was quite sure it was a prank call. Summit only has four full-time employees, but we have about eighty highly trained instructors—who all happen to be great pranksters. I thought it was one of them pulling my leg, so I went along.

"Oh, sure, Ron. I've been thinking a lot about leisure, joy, and celebrating life lately."

After about ten minutes of bantering, I said:

"Okay, I give. Who is this, anyway?"

The voice on the other end said, "Pardon?"

I said, "C'mon, I've got to get up at five. You get extra points for this one. Who is this?"

"Pardon?"

I finally said (though I still can't believe it), "C'mon, you jerk, who is this?"

When I heard the third "Pardon?", I knew I was in trouble. A little flustered, I said, "This isn't really Ron Wilson from David C. Cook Publishing Company, is it?"

At his fourth "Pardon?" I froze, overwhelmed with embarrassment.

After a few minutes of explaining and apologizing, I asked if we could still have lunch. Fortunately, Ron is very gracious.

That lunch began a whole new season for me. I had kept journals for over ten years, but had never published anything except articles. Ron's bold confidence and insistent encouragement over the next two years resulted in *When I Relax I Feel Guilty* being published in 1979.

I remember finishing the final manuscript at 5:30 in the morning. My feeble prayer as I mailed it off was, "O Lord, please let it sell at least eight copies!" (I figured each member of my family would want one, anyway.) The fact that it has sold over 100,000 copies and is in its twelfth printing still astounds me.

But that wasn't the most significant result. At least two vital occurrences took place in my life because of that book. One was my discovery that I had a "blessed rage to write" as well as live. Writing, I soon discovered, was a way in which I could *taste life twice.* It gave me time and opportunity to savor life again from different and unique angles. I was invited to go behind the appearances to unwrap the essence of my experiences.

The privilege of relishing the substance of time and experience for a second or third time led to another turning point: I realized the incredible importance of making a commitment to joy. In the first book I quoted

Swiss psychologist Paul Tournier as saying, "Most people spend their entire lives indefinitely *preparing* to live." I realized that I was guilty of the very problem I was trying to point out to others. I was putting off joy until my circumstances improved.

Some time later, after the book was published, I discovered Nehemiah 8:10, "The joy of the Lord is *your strength*." No truths are simple, especially those of Scripture. But as we pursue them and *participate* in them more fully, they begin to reveal to us a life deeper and more integrated than we ever could have known otherwise.

My rage to live was real, but I had, without knowing or intending it, put a lid on it by saying to myself, "When I am strong, then I'll be joyful. When the pain eases, then I'll be joyful." I had enough excuses to last a lifetime.

The problem was reality. The pain didn't subside. And I had placed myself in the position of waiting until things got better, waiting until I knew more of God, waiting until I had enough strength to be joyful.

But through this profound and simple passage from Nehemiah, God reminded me again and again that I cannot choose to be strong, but I can choose to be joyful. And when I am willing to do that, strength will follow.

The connection between joy and strength had a stronger impact on my life than I first realized. The Bible says if we *know* the truth it will set us free (John 8:32). It seems to me, however, that there is something qualitatively different between knowing and just believing. *Knowing* in both the Old and New Testaments implies intimacy, deep understanding, and experience. It implies an element of participation beyond mere cerebral assent. It is belief which has matured and taken root, and has been translated from mere cognition to a new kind of power.

I began not only to *choose* joy, but to explore its meaning and integrity. I discovered that joy was much different and much deeper than I'd imagined.

The joy which I began to discover was radically different from the kind of joy (i.e., happiness) I'd known before. Above all else, this joy did *not* depend on circumstances. In fact, it was cited most frequently in Scripture as being in *spite* of circumstances.

> *Though* the fig tree does not bud
>     and there are no grapes on the vines,
> *though* the olive crop fails
>     and the fields produce no food,
> *though* there are no sheep in the pen
>     and no cattle in the stalls,
> *yet* I will rejoice in the Lord,
>     *I will be joyful* in God my Savior.
> The Sovereign Lord *is my strength;*
>     he makes my feet like the feet of a deer,
>     he enables me to go on the heights.
>
> HABAKKUK 3:17-19

I began to realize that it wasn't my imposed limitations that held me back as much as my *perception* of those limitations. It wasn't the pain that was thwarting me as much as it was my *attitude* toward the pain. I realized that though the difficulties were undeniably real, and would remain so for the rest of my life, I had the opportunity to *choose* a new freedom and joy if I wanted to.

I read that:

• through Christ we have not only obtained access to this immense stuff that we call grace, but even more

than that, we can share his very life and even *rejoice* in our sufferings *now.* (Romans 5)
• to my astonishment, I should consider it all *joy* when I am overwhelmed by trials (James 1).
• I am not to be surprised by the ordeals which we must all endure in order to "prove us" (I Peter 4:12).
• my joy could be restored (Psalm 51:12) and increased (II Corinthians 1:24).

The Book I was reading even went so far as to say in bold black-and-white that the *will* of God for me was to "be joyful always; pray continually; and give thanks in *all* circumstances" (I Thessalonians 5:16-18). Otherwise I am in danger of quenching the Spirit (v. 19).

I had always believed that all these statements in Scripture were true, but I realized that they would have to take on new levels of reality for me. The possibility of joy in the *midst* of all this seemed remote, but the journey had begun.

# PART TWO
# JOY IS A CHOICE

*The surest mark of a Christian is not faith, or even love, but joy.*

*Samuel M. Shoemaker*

# Choose Joy

*You and I were created for joy, and if we miss it, we miss the reason for our existence. . . . If our joy is honest joy, it must somehow be congruous with human tragedy. This is the test of joy's integrity: is it compatible with pain? . . . Only the heart that hurts has a right to joy.*[1]

LEWIS SMEDES

*Now*
*there was only the morning*
*and the dancing man of the broken tomb.*
*The story says*
*he dances still.*
*That is why*
*down to this day*
*we lean over the beds of our babies*
*and in the seconds before sleep*
*tell the story of the undying dancing man*
*so the dream of Jesus will carry them to dawn.*[2]

JOHN SHEA

THE WORD *HAPPINESS* comes from the same root as the word *happening*, suggesting that happiness is based on something happening to us. Happiness is circumstantial. If I pay off my car, I'm happy. If I get a new shirt, I'm happy. If my friends say nice things, I'm happy.

There is nothing wrong with happiness. It's wonderful. The only problem is that it's based on circumstances, and circumstances have a tendency to shift.

Most people who live with chronic pain or chronic problems have a hard time being happy. That is to be expected. Although there are moments of laughter, nothing seems to stay.

Joy, on the other hand, is something which defies circumstances and occurs in spite of difficult situations. Whereas happiness is a feeling, joy is an attitude. A posture. A position. A place. As Paul Sailhamer says, "Joy is that deep settled confidence that God is in control of every area of my life."

I have a plaque, sent to me during the most difficult period of my entire life, that says the following:

> *Tim,*
> *Trust me*
> *I have everything*
> *under control!*
> *Jesus*

It was sent by a friend who knew that I needed that reminder. Ironically, the glass got broken during shipping. I have never replaced the glass because, to me, the message is even stronger behind shattered glass. We can know a joy that transcends circumstances and is of a substance and faith that is beyond situations.

If we are to have this kind of joy in our lives, we must first discover what it looks like. It is not a feeling; it is a *choice*. It is not based upon circumstances; it is based upon attitude. It is free, but it is not cheap. It is the by-product of a growing relationship with Jesus Christ. It is a promise, not a deal. It is available to us when we make ourselves available to him. It is something that we can receive by invitation and by choice. It requires commitment, courage, and endurance.

When Paul listed the fruit of the Spirit, he named joy second, reminding us that *joy* is a very high priority in the Christian walk. A friend once asked if it were possible that the listing meant that joy was the second most important virtue in the Christian faith. It's worth considering. Another friend looked at the first three—love, joy, and peace—and commented, "I never realized that it was joy that holds love and peace together."

I am certain that joy is far more important than any of us has ever imagined. And I am certain that it is far more available than any of us has ever dreamed.

## Joy Is a Choice

Pain is inevitable, but misery is optional. We cannot avoid pain, but we can avoid joy. God has given us such immense freedom that he will allow us to be as miserable as we want to be.

I know some people who spend their entire lives practicing being unhappy, diligently pursuing joyless-ness. They get more mileage from having people feel sorry for them than from choosing to live out their lives in the context of joy.

Joy is simple (not to be confused with easy). At any moment in life we have at least two options, and one of them is to choose an attitude of gratitude, a posture of grace, a commitment to joy.

There is no question that life is difficult. In fact, it has been said that God promises four things: peace, power, purpose, and TROUBLE. For example, in John 16:33 Jesus reminds us quite boldly that in the world there will be trouble. There will be tribulation, but we are not merely to endure it but to "be of good cheer," for he has overcome the world.

Many of us have only gotten half the message. We recognize the difficulty of life and drearily drag ourselves through each day, mumbling about our burdens. (I've heard it said that "some Christians have just enough Christianity to make them miserable.") It can be different—but the choice is ours.

## Joy Doesn't Depend on Circumstances

As I learned after my accident, I could not live by the maxim "When I get stronger, then I'll be joyful." It's an attitude so many people share, agreeing to be joyful as soon as circumstances improve.
• As soon as the kids are grown, you'll see me shine.
• As soon as I get a better job, I'll be more productive.
• As soon as I lose weight, then I'll be truly joyful.
• As soon as the car gets fixed, as soon as the bills get paid, as soon as, as soon as, as soon as, as soon as.

I know people who have fallen into the trap of endlessly putting off joy. For complex, and perhaps even justifiable, reasons they have chosen to avoid the wonderful responsibility of joy in the here and now.

## Joy Is Free, But Not Cheap

In our society you can buy almost anything. Security, comfort, convenience, status, and perhaps even momentary happiness can be purchased. I contend, however, that true joy has a different kind of price tag. It always has been and always will be free. We do not have to move anywhere or change anything to find it. Like grace, it is itself an inexpressible gift, available to all who would choose to partake.

But there is no such thing as *cheap* joy. Joy often costs pain and suffering. True joy isn't found at the end of a rainbow. It isn't captured at the top of the ladder of success. Its price tag is faithfulness, endurance, and perhaps sorrow. It has been suggested that our cup of joy can only be as deep as our cup of sorrow.

Joy has so much to do with how we see and hear and experience the world. It is not to be grasped, but given away. It is not to be contained, but shared. Joy has more to do with who we are than what we have, more to do with the healthiness of our attitude than with the health of our body. Joy, above all else, is a selfless quality which is magnified when it is shared and minimized when it is selfishly grasped.

The following story is well-known, but I hope you'll agree that it can stand the retelling.

There were once two men, both seriously ill, in the same small room of a great hospital. Quite a small room, just large enough for the pair of them—two beds, two bedside lockers, a door opening on the hall, and one window looking out on the world.

One of the men, as part of his treatment, was allowed to sit up in bed for an hour in the afternoon (something to do with draining the fluid from his lungs), and his bed was next to the window.

But the other man had to spend all his time flat on his back—and both of them had to be kept quiet and still. Which was the reason they were in the small room by themselves, and they were grateful for peace and privacy—none of the bustle and clatter and prying eyes of the general ward for them.

Of course, one of the disadvantages of their condition was that they weren't allowed to do much: no reading, no radio, certainly no television—they just had to keep quiet and still, just the two of them.

Well, they used to talk for hours and hours—about their wives, their children, their homes, their jobs, their hobbies, their childhood, what they did during the war, where they'd been on vacations—all that sort of thing. Every afternoon, when the man in the bed next to the window was propped up for his hour, he would pass the time by describing what he could see outside. And the other man began to live for those hours.

The window apparently overlooked a park, with a lake, where there were ducks and swans, children throwing them bread and sailing model boats, and young lovers walking hand in hand beneath the trees, and there were flowers and stretches of grass, games of softball, people taking their ease in the sunshine, and right at the back, behind the fringe of trees, a fine view of the city skyline.

The man on his back would listen to all of this, enjoying every minute—how a child nearly fell into the lake, how beautiful the girls were in their summer dresses, then an exciting ball game, or a boy playing with his puppy. It got to the place that he could almost see what was happening outside.

Then one fine afternoon, when there was some sort of parade, the thought struck him: Why should the man next to the window have all the pleasure of seeing what was going on? Why shouldn't he get the chance?

He felt ashamed, and tried not to think like that, but the more he tried, the worse he wanted a change. He'd do anything!

In a few days, he had turned sour. *He* should be by the window. And he brooded, and couldn't sleep, and grew even more seriously ill—which none of the doctors understood.

One night as he stared at the ceiling, the other man suddenly woke up, coughing and choking, the fluid congesting in his lungs, his hands groping for the button that would bring the night nurse running. But the man watched without moving.

The coughing racked the darkness—on and on—choked off—then stopped—the sound of breathing stopped—and the man continued to stare at the ceiling.

In the morning the day nurse came in with water for their baths and found the other man dead. They took away his body, quietly, no fuss.

As soon as it seemed decent, the man asked if he could be moved to the bed next to the window. And they moved him, tucked him in, and made him quite comfortable, and left him alone to be quiet and still.

The minute they'd gone, he propped himself up on one elbow, painfully and laboriously, and looked out the window.

It faced a blank wall.[3]

G. W. TARGET

I've known people whose lives have "faced a blank wall" and yet they made it sound beautiful. Their courage was evidenced in little commitments they made every day, little acts of gratitude and wonder—in spite of their circumstances. Like the first man in the story, they made life come alive for those around them.

## Joy Is a Choice

The first man deliberately chose to introduce joy into a dismal situation. True joy wants to give itself away, and is magnified by doing so.

The second man illustrates the desperate need for circumstances to produce happiness. He was so desperate that he even allowed it to cost him his friend, and only in the end did he realize that the joy he had was independent of circumstances.

## Joy Is Based on Being

Our country was founded on the pursuit of happiness, grew and developed in the pursuit of excellence, and has now come to be dominated by the pursuit of trivia. William McNamara opens his book, *The Human Adventure,* by saying that he believes that all the evils of this age have their basis in superficiality of one sort or another.

We are a nation of people consumed by having. We want to have not only material things, but facts. We want to have knowledge. We want to have information. We even want to have love and inspiration. We want to have happiness and have abundance. Ownership seems to be the king of virtues, no matter what the commodity, and yet we are a society of notoriously unhappy people; lonely, anxious, depressed, dependent.

By now we should have learned that unrestricted satisfaction of all desires is not conducive to well-being. We know this to be true for our children, and yet sometimes we fail to recognize its truth in our own lives. Greed and peace preclude each other.

One of the problems is that we have forgotten that God created us as *beings,* not as *doings.* Our goal should be to *be* much, not *have* much. In Erich Fromm's insightful *To Have or to Be?* he delineates the difference between the having mode and being mode. The having mode is the consuming and possessing mode. It is based on the formula: I am equals what I have and what I consume. The being mode, on the other hand, is both liberated and liberating. It is the simple recognition that one cannot have knowledge or have love.

> To say, "I have love for you," is meaningless. Love is not a thing that one can have, but a process, an inner activity that one is the subject of. I can love, I can be in love, but in loving I have . . . nothing. In fact, the less I have, the more I can love.[4]
>
> ERICH FROMM

Eugene Peterson's modern English rendition of Galatians 2 is relevant to our discussion of the importance of being.

> Have some of you noticed that we are not yet perfect? And are you ready to make the accusation that since people like me, who seek to be justified by Christ, aren't perfectly virtuous, Christ must therefore be an accessory to sin? The accusation is frivolous. If I was "trying to be good," I would be reconstructing the same old barn that I tore down and acting as a charlatan. What actually took place is this: I tried keeping the rules and working my head off to please God, and it didn't work; so I quit so that I could simply be, so I could live in harmony with God. Christ's life showed me how and enabled me to do it. I identified myself completely with him; indeed I have been crucified with Christ. My ego is no longer central. It is no longer important that I appear righteous before you or have your good opinion, and I am no longer driven [even] to please God. Christ lives in me: the life you see me living is lived by faith in the son of God who loved me and gave himself for me. I am not going to go back on that. Is it not clear to you that to go back to that old rule-keeping, peer-pleasing religion would be an abandonment of everything personal and free in relationship with God? I refuse to do that, to repudiate God's grace. If a living relationship with God came by rule keeping, then Christ died gratuitously. We are justified by faith in Christ. Justification means being put together the way we are supposed to be. Made right—not improved, not decorated, not veneered, not patched up, but justified. Our fundamental being is set in right relationship with God. This setting right is not impersonal fixing; it is personal reconciliation. We are never right in ourselves, but only in response to and as a result of God working in and through us.[5]

This is the source of true joy.

# Bite the Bullet

*God has given us two incredible things: absolutely awesome ability and freedom of choice. The tragedy is that, for the most part, many of us have refused them both.* FRANK DONNELLY

*If your happiness [or health] depends on what somebody else says [or does], I guess you do have a problem.*
RICHARD BACH

*You will surely forget your trouble,*
  *recalling it only as waters gone by.*
*Life will be brighter than noonday,*
  *and darkness will become like morning.*
*You will be secure, because there is hope;*
  *you will look about you and take your rest in safety.*
JOB 11:16-18

THERE WAS TO BE ONE more critical piece in the puzzle which evolved into a turning point. It had to do with choice. I knew I had the freedom and power to choose my attitude toward my situation, but I felt I had little control over what was actually going on in my body.

63

The doctors had told me that my situation was progressive and deteriorating. I would go to them and ask, "How am I doing?"

The news usually wasn't all that good, so I would ask the next obvious question. "What can you do about it?" In a sense, they were in control of my health. And what I usually wanted, and received, was symptom suppression. What prescription can you give me to relieve the pain?

Without realizing it, I had gone into a stall where I was basically subduing and enduring the pain. I didn't know I had another choice. I became more cautious in physical activity because one doctor told me that if I hit a doorjamb wrong, I would become a paraplegic, because my vertebrae were so unstable.

The more cautiously I lived my life, the more intense the pain became. I knew myself well enough to know that I don't live well cautiously. I simply existed from one prescription to the next, hoping that the doctors would eventually find the right combination that would make me better.

I lived with low-level discouragement and low-grade unhappiness, which I would bolster occasionally with some of the newly discovered joy I was finding and experiencing.

\*       \*       \*

It was a busy afternoon at the Summit office. I had been sitting all day, going over papers and records with a dear friend and saint, Vern Frederickson. Vern is one of those rare individuals who, upon retirement, gave his life to full-time voluntary ministry. He and Marnie, his wife, bolstered up many programs like ours with their time, enthusiasm, and tangible contributions.

I was a little slow and stiff getting up out of my chair, and Vern saw that I was in pain.

"When was the last time you saw the doctor?"

It was an awkward question, because at the time I was occupationally and physically uninsurable. When insurance companies found out about my physical situation and my vocation of working with a mountaineering program, they considered me too much of a risk. Their rates became so ridiculously high that, on my salary, I chose to be without insurance for a while. Because of this, I had spread out my visits to doctors, seeing them only enough to maintain prescriptions.

But when Vern perceives a problem, he attacks it with a sense of abandon. Forty minutes later he told me that I had a doctor's appointment the next afternoon with a leading orthopedic specialist in Los Angeles.

Dr. Albert Meyer looked his role. I was calmed by his warmth and presence, and his snow-white hair gave him an added aura of wisdom.

I'd been instructed to bring all my previous X rays, and the doctor placed them in order on lighted screens. After studying them carefully for five or ten minutes, he turned to me. With a gentle smile and a slight twinkle in his eye, he said, "You're kind of screwed up, aren't you?"

We both laughed. Then he asked, with the gentleness of a real artist, "What would you like me to do?"

I said, "Well, I want to know what you can do about it, I guess."

"Do you mean medically?"

"Yes, I suppose so."

For the next thirty minutes I watched as Dr. Meyer brought in a number of different colleagues to look at the X rays. They spoke quietly to each other, pointed at the X rays, and made comments among themselves.

Finally he dismissed the others and turned back to me. "You said you'd like to know what we can do for you medically. Correct?"

"Yes!"

"Not a darn thing!"

I was taken aback, but somehow, the way he said it, it didn't sound like a negative remark.

"The damage has been done, son. There's nothing that we can do at this time. Surgery wouldn't help, because many of the vertebrae have already fused themselves arthritically."

"What does this mean?" I asked.

"Well, all I can tell you is that everybody has to live with something. What you are going to have to live with is pain—but it's not the end of the world. You're still blessed with many things, such as movement."

"What do you suggest I do?"

"I suggest that you bite the bullet and live to be a hundred!"

It was the most powerful sign of hope I'd had from a doctor in a long time.

"Well, what *can't* I do?"

After a moment's thought he said, "Well, there's so much damage in your neck that I wouldn't recommend painting eaves."

"I hate to paint. What else?"

"Son, listen to me carefully. The damage has been done. The worst is over. You will have to live with pain, but that's a small price to pay for life. My recommendation is that you live your life as fully and richly as possible." Then he said it again. "Bite the bullet and live to be a hundred. As far as I can tell, you can do whatever the pain will allow you to do."

Some may say they're not sure if this was good news or bad news. To me it was nothing less than *great* news, offering incredible hope.

"Dr. Meyers, may I ask you one more question?"

"Of course."

"Does this mean that the ball is in *my* court? From here on out it's up to me?"

"Absolutely. The choice is yours."

He turned and left as quietly as he had come in. I muttered a quiet thank-you, both to him and to Him. Then I gathered up my X rays and ran down the eight flights of stairs, ignoring the elevator.

I left downtown Los Angeles with a new lease on life, a resurgent hope for the future, and a new commitment to live life again with a sense of abandonment, no matter what the consequences.

As strange as it may seem, up to that point I hadn't known I had a choice. I hadn't realized that my health was in my hands, not the doctors'. I was responsible for who I was to be and how healthy I could become.

The process put me back in the present tense. It changed my if to yes. It was a genesis moment when I discovered again that I was in control of my pain, my future, my attitudes, my life.

I arrived home with a new level of acceptance for my circumstances. I was not unmindful of the seriousness of my situation, but I was overwhelmed by a festive hope and was no longer trapped in the cycle of fear, depression, and cautious panic. Deep down I knew I had a good chance of beating the odds, and I relished the challenge.

It was shortly after that that I was given a copy of Norman Cousins's *Anatomy of an Illness.* Is it not amazing that there are so many "coincidences" for a

Christian? Cousins's book emphasizes both the importance of accepting responsibility for our own health and—strangely enough—the vital importance of laughter. Nehemiah 8:10 was coming back to me in a new dimension.

> Scientific research has established the existence of endorphins in the human brain—a substance very much like morphine in its molecular structure and effects. It is the body's own anesthesia and a relaxant and helps human beings to sustain pain.[1]
>
> NORMAN COUSINS

Although it is still not known exactly how endorphins are released, there is evidence to support the thought that they are released by such things as exercise and, yes, laughter.

It has long been recognized that negative attitudes such as worry can produce negative physical effects, such as ulcers. Cousins simply surmised that the opposite might also be true—that positive emotions, such as laughter and joy, would produce positive chemical reactions in the body. A cheerful heart *is* truly good medicine (Proverbs 17:22).

Cousins's miraculous cure from a fatal collagen disease, through high doses of laughter and high dosages of vitamin C, is strong evidence. And the change in my own life has been, for me, further verification of the importance of personal responsibility for one's health, including a cheerful heart.

> There are only two ways to approach life—as a victim or as a gallant fighter—and you must decide if you want to act or react. . . . A lot of people forget that.[2]
>
> MERLE SHAIN

I had allowed myself to step into the victim mentality without wanting it or knowing it. But through a gentle doctor, our Lord again "turned my mourning into dancing, and my sackcloth into joy" (Psalm 30:11).

# Mere Life

*I danced on Friday when the sky turned black*
*Oh, it's hard to dance with the devil on your back*
*They buried My body and they thought I'd gone*
*But I am the dance and the dance goes on*
*Dance, dance, wherever you may be*
*I am the Lord of the dance, said He*
*And I will lead you all wherever you may be*
*I'll lead you all in the dance, said He.*[1]

SYDNEY CARTER

*Remember all those things we used to blame on the devil? And*
*all those things we left up to God? Now it's a hundred times*
*more complicated. We must become new men or be satisfied as*
*we are. Either way we risk tragedy.*[2]

SISTER CORITA

A FEW YEARS AGO I HAD A CONVERSATION with an
elderly gentleman who radiated a special presence and
a strong and genuine serenity. Somewhere in the midst
of our conversation he said, "As I get older, I seem to
place less importance on material things." And then,

71

after a pause, he continued, "Come to think of it, I place less importance on importance."

There is something very special about life, but many people—in fact, most—miss it. In our overemphasis on "important" things, we often overlook the intrinsic value of life itself. We have confused form with essence. We have placed our supreme value on surface things and have forgotten the substance. We have begun to believe the radio and TV commercials and have put so many overlays on our life that we can no longer see the fine-grained texture of everyday life itself, the mystery of the ordinary.

Have we forgotten how special Wednesdays can be? Have we forgotten how different November is, when the trees appear in the lean economy of leafless elegance? Have we somehow fallen into the rut where we think that all Mondays are dreary or that February is a difficult month? Have we gotten trapped into comparisons and ingratitudes? Are we in the habit of always putting off an experience until we can afford it? Or until the time is right? Or until we know how to do it? Procrastinating over the joy of being alive is one of the greatest burglars of life I know.

> The truth is that life is delicious, horrible, charming, sweet, bitter and that is everything.
>
> ANATOLE FRANCE

Now is as good as any time to jump in.

Our society has inundated us with the importance of importance. We have been conditioned to believe in the big, the fast, the expensive and the far away. I'm still convinced that if you have to move even ten inches from where you are now in order to be happy, you never will be. Life becomes precious and more special to us when we look for the little everyday miracles and get excited again about the privilege of simply being human.

Awhile ago I turned down an invitation to a seminar. The speaker was famous, and what he was planning to talk on promised to be profound. Instead, I chose to stay at home and have a long, drawn-out breakfast with my family. After that, there were extensive wrestling matches in the living room between my boys and me. The rest of the day was spent puttering around our little home. A drain pipe needed fixing, Zac's bike needed adjustment, Josh's birthday present had fallen into ill repair, and the two rear doors on our station wagon had been tied together with rope for weeks. It turned out to be an absolutely glorious day of doing little things. Simple things. Just enjoying the immense privilege of being alive.

Two days later I spoke with friends who had been at the conference. It was good, they said, but not quite as profound as everyone had anticipated. Somehow in the midst of our conversation, I couldn't help feeling that I had chosen the more significant experience.

This time called life is far more sacred and special than any of us can ever imagine. Our task, or should I say our privilege, is to become aware of it and to participate as deeply and as fully as we are capable. We often put a false barrier between what we call the secular and the sacred, limiting the way that God can touch us and express himself through us.

There is a powerful story of a young man who was desperately seeking God. He sought out a wise old man who lived in a nearby beach house and posed the question: "Old man, how can I see God?" The old man who obviously knew God at a depth few of us experience, pondered the question for a very long time. At last he responded quietly: "Young man, I am not sure that I can help you—for you see, I have a very different problem. I cannot *not* see him."

Life. The temptation is always to reduce it to size. A bowl of cherries. A rat race. Amino acids. Even to call it a mystery smacks of reductionism. It is *the* mystery.

As far as anybody seems to know, the vast majority of things in the universe do not have whatever life is. Sticks, stones, stars, space—they simply *are*. A few things *are* and are somehow aware of it. They have broken through into Something, or Something has broken through into them. Even a jellyfish, a butternut squash. They're in it with us. We're all in it together, or it in us. Life is *it*. Life is *with*.

After lecturing learnedly on miracles, a great theologian was asked to give a specific example of one. "There is only one miracle," he answered. "It is life."

Have you wept at anything during the past year?
Has your heart beat faster at the sight of young beauty?
Have you thought seriously about the fact that someday you are going to die?
More often than not do you really *listen* when people are speaking to you instead of just waiting for your turn to speak?
Is there anybody you know in whose place, if one of you had to suffer great pain, you would volunteer yourself?

If your answer to all or most of these questions is No, the chances are that you're dead. [3]

FREDERICK BUECHNER

Whether one looks at a star, a child, a moment of sorrow, or a time of gladness, blessed is the ordinary. In an attempt to distill for myself and others the good that sometimes eludes us as we are caught in the pressures to achieve and succeed, I believe the small moment is the carrier of God's most endearing gift, and that it must not be permitted to slip away unsavored and unappreciated. . . . If one accepts each day as a gift from the Father's hand, one may sometimes hear a voice saying, "Open it. I invite you to share with me in these little appointments with myself as we try to unwrap the hidden beauties in an ordinary day." [4]

GERHARD FROST

You and I are alive. It is a privilege that none of us can fully comprehend. It needn't have been so. The grace of everyday living is a gift.

## Life Is Sacred

Grace is free, but it certainly isn't cheap. You may have read the story of David Rothenberg in a newspaper a few years ago. It was a tragic story of a father who, in a fit of rage, went into his son's room, poured kerosene all over the room and all over the tiny boy, and lit him on fire. In God's difficult grace, David somehow lived through it, though ninety-five percent of his body was covered with third-degree burns. To this day, he has virtually no skin. It is estimated that David will have approximately 5,000 operations in his lifetime. Each year they have to open him up so that he can grow. Along with a few saints and poets, David Rothenberg is aware of the greatest miracle of all: LIFE ITSELF. At the age of 7, he had the audacity to say:

*I am alive!*

*I am alive!*

*I am alive!*

*I didn't miss out on living! And that is wonderful enough for me.*

75

Perhaps the thing that creates the deepest sadness in me is to watch people continually miss the miracle of being alive. I see people constantly who wander through each day, almost forcing themselves, it seems *not* to experience life. Like flies crawling across the roof of the Sistine Chapel, we're unable to see the beauty and grandeur at our feet. But do we all have to experience tragedy before we can see life's majesty? I certainly hope not.

Perhaps the most important thing that I have learned in my journey with pain is the intrinsic value of life itself—the sacredness of each unrepeatable moment. To partake of it is sheer gift; none of us did anything to deserve it. The most tangible form of grace itself is the substance of our normal everyday life. Perhaps it has been worth all the pain just to learn this one blessed lesson.

Helen Keller is one of my great heroines. Though struck deaf and blind at the age of two, she later said, "Life is either a daring adventure . . . or nothing at all."

I, who cannot see, find hundreds of things to interest me through mere touch. I feel the delicate symmetry of a leaf. I pass my hands lovingly about the smooth skin of a silver birch or the rough shaggy bark of a pine. I feel the delightful, velvety texture of a flower and discover its remarkable convolutions and something of the miracle of nature is revealed to me. Occasionally, if I'm very fortunate, I can place my hand gently on a small tree and feel the happy quiver of a bird in full song. At times, my heart cries out, longing to see these things. But if I can get so much pleasure in mere touch, how much more beauty must be revealed by sight? Yet, those who have eyes apparently see little. The panorama of color and action which fill the world are taken for granted. It is a great pity that in the world of light the

gift of sight is used only as a mere convenience, rather than as a means of adding fullness.[5]
                                    HELEN KELLER

Too many people walk through life with gloves and a raincoat on, refusing to observe and *experience* the beauty and the wonder of the world around them. So many have forgotten the privilege of not only earthly delights, but also of our unearthly purpose. I see so many, including myself, who take our divine privilege for granted. Each day has its own distinctness and its own inexhaustibility. And yet how few realize it. Just because we take something for granted, doesn't mean it still isn't miraculous. Perhaps nothing is really ordinary.

The central theme of Thornton Wilder's Pulitzer Prize winning *Our Town* is the bittersweet music of ordinary life. The play focuses around the small ordinary town of Grover. It could be the story of any one of us; the setting could be the very town we live in. With subtle brilliance, Wilder underscores the blessedness of everyday living. The very wonder of life itself and the tragic reminder that many fail to recognize until its too late reaches a high note when Emily dies far too young in childbirth. The next scene is, for me, the most memorable in the play. Emily asks for the privilege of going back to see life one last time. Although the other ghosts discourage her, she insists and ends up going back to her twelfth birthday. There she views her own life through the thin veil that separates life and death. She is painfully startled to realize that people don't recognize how short and sacred life is. She pleads her case but no one can hear her—except us. Except us. What Emily notices most are the simple things—the smell of coffee, the feel of a starched dress, the simple delicate taste of a morning meal, a touch, a look, an ever swift passing moment of tenderness. No one can read or see this play without a catch of breath, a quiet pause during which we are haltingly grateful again for the gift of life itself. As Emily says, "Oh, earth, you are too wonderful for anyone to realize you. Did any human beings ever realize life (and how wonderful it is) while they live it? Every, every minute."

So many people seem to treat their faith as if it were an artificial limb that they strap on each day. Though it helps them stumble along, it never really becomes a part of them. Whatever happened to that holy wonder, that appetite for the sacred? Have we grown blind to the sacredness of everyday things and of everyday people? Where is our appetite for stillness which, as T. S. Eliot says, "is the turning point, is where the dance is." What are we waiting for?

There are fathers waiting until other obligations are less demanding to become acquainted with their sons. . . . There are mothers who sincerely intend to be more attentive to their daughers. . . . There are husbands and wives who are going to be more understanding. . . . But time does not draw people closer. . . .

When in the world are we going to begin to live as if we understood that this is life? This is our time, our day . . . and it is passing. What are we waiting for? [6]

RICHARD L. EVANS

## Life Is Short

Paul Weber was one of our brightest and most talented Summit Expedition instructors. He was twenty-six, strong, an incredible athlete, vitally and vividly committed to Jesus Christ. He and his soon-to-be wife planned to travel all over New Zealand and Australia on passes that he had saved while working at a travel agency. One evening we sat and talked together for four hours. A week later Paul died in a tragic accident.

Life is short—for some it's even shorter than it's "supposed" to be. Countless books have been written and lectures given on why such things happen. That is beyond me. But the question in the midst of all this is how can we, knowing that life is so incredibly delicious and short lived, still continue to live bland, insipid lives? How can we, seeing such evidence every day in the papers, continue to waste the days that God has given us? How can we keep on indefinitely preparing to live, knowing that each day comes but once in human history?

Zac will be eleven in a few weeks. It's the only eleventh birthday he will ever have. Joshua just turned eight—he will only be eight once in his lifetime. If I miss it, I miss it. There are no instant replays, no video playbacks in this time called life.

Last night I walked past Joshua's bedroom. His room was dark, except for the light from a tiny lamp that sits on the table next to his bed. There he was, propped up on two pillows, tucked underneath his Star Wars blanket, wearing a stocking cap to bed. The cap was white with blue and red inscriptions and a little white tassle on top. I couldn't help but stop and absorb the tenderness of it all. As I shared that moment with Pam a few moments later in the kitchen, she said the same thing I was thinking: "He won't be wearing that to bed for very long, so we might as well enjoy those brief moments now."

It's been said that as we get older, we don't regret the things that we did do, but only those things that we failed or forgot to do. How many of those wonderful, brief capsules of time do I miss each day, I wonder?

Choose life!
  Only that and always!
  At whatever risk.
To let life leak out . . .
  To let it wear away
  By the mere passage of time . . .
To withhold giving it and spending it . . .
  Is to choose nothing!

SISTER HELEN KELLY

At times I grow embarrassed when I realize how deaf I am to life's symphony, for if God speaks to us anywhere, I think it is in our daily lives. I wonder how much of God's grace I experience . . . and how much I'm capable of experiencing.

Pam and I recently enjoyed going through old scrapbooks and photographs. The photographs from our wedding made our hearts surge with gladness. We looked at pictures of the kids when they were first born. There were wonderful shots from our vacation last summer, and the incredible eighteen-inch trout that Zac caught. We saw pictures of Joshua when he could barely sit up in the rocking chair and when he was first learning to walk. Those moments will never come again.

—how fortunate are you and i,whose home
is timelessness: we who have wandered down
from fragrant mountains of eternal now

to frolic in such mysteries as birth
and death a day(or maybe even less)[7]

E. E. CUMMINGS

I don't know how much string is left on my ball of twine. There are no guarantees as to how long any of us

80

will live, but I know full well that I would rather make my days count than merely count my days. I want to live each one of them as close to the core of life as possible, experiencing as much of God and my family and friends as I am capable. Since life is inevitably too short, for all of us, I know full well that I want to enjoy it as much as I can, no matter what the circumstances are.

## Life Is Funny

I enjoy laughing. I believe that laughter is a sacred sound to our God. I also believe that it has an incredible capacity to heal our bodies, our minds, and our spirits. Wisdom down through the ages has reminded us that "a cheerful heart is good medicine." (Proverbs 17:22)

*Are you fun to live with?* Do you approach life with a sense of humor? Are you able to look at the light side of things in spite of difficulties?

One day I asked a friend what she thought the five most important ingredients were to being a quality human being. After a long and thoughtful pause, Norma said, "Humor, love, responsibility, courage, and humor." I tried to point out that she had already said humor, but she informed me that she meant exactly what she had said. She felt strongly, that at least two of the five prime ingredients for being a quality human being are a good sense of humor.

Our ability to laugh and enjoy life is a good mirror of our health. Some years ago I taught a special class at Azusa Pacific University which had optimum health as its primary focus. I discovered in the process that the word *health* means wholeness. So the primary theme of the course was an attempt to discover for each of us how we could become most whole, most alive in Christ.

At the end of the semester I asked the class to tell me who they thought the five best examples of wholeness were. Whose life gave this concept the most meaning to them? They convened in small groups, and when I finally called for their response, they gave me a memorable answer. They unanimously chose Tre Bernhard as the greatest living example of wholeness that they ever knew.

Tre was in our class. Some serious congenital problems had left her with only one leg that could do no more than hold a shoe. She had a total of six stubby fingers. But if you were to meet her, you would most likely agree with the class, because the two most predominant features about Tre are her incredible compassion and her lively sense of humor. Tre had been through hardships even worse than her physical handicaps. She had lived a life that would devastate most people, yet she *chose* to transcend the situation and give to the world a tangible sense of love and humor that changed more than one life, including my own.

Humor has the unshakable ability to break life up into little pieces and make it liveable. Laughter adds richness, texture, and color to otherwise ordinary days. It is a gift, a choice, a discipline, and an art.

I'm convinced that life is rather funny, even amidst all its tragic realities. I collect everything that I can find that will make me laugh and tickle others, as well. When I'm given the privilege to speak to groups, one of the most important elements for me is that we laugh some together.

So I keep a bright green folder and I put into it things that I think might tickle people into the wonder of being alive. For example, there is the collection of thoughts on bad days:

You know it's going to be a bad day when . . .
—You call your answering service and they tell you it's none of your business.
—You put your pants on backwards—and they fit better.
—Your horn goes off accidentally and remains stuck as you follow a group of Hell's Angels on the freeway.
—You sink your teeth into a beautiful steak and they stay there.

Then there is a collection on aging.

You know you are getting older when:
—Your back goes out more than you do.
—Your knees buckle, but your belt won't.
—You get winded playing chess.
—You sit in a rocking chair and can't make it go.
—You turn out the light for economic rather than romantic reasons.
—Dialing long distance wears you out.

I read these one evening at a seminar, and a spritely older lady came up afterward. She said she knew that she was getting older when one day she reached down to tie her shoes and actually said to herself: "I wonder if there is anything else I can do while I'm down here." Life really is fun, if we only give it a chance. Countless moments of serendipity are constantly alive to us and inviting us to participate, if we but have eyes to see, ears to hear, and hearts to respond. Everyday life has its own hidden comedy. As John Powell said "Blessed is he who has learned to laugh at himself, for he shall never cease to be entertained." When we can laugh at ourselves and our own situations and the life around us, it literally produces physiological and chemical changes in our bodies that bring about a greater sense of vitality, health, and even healing.

One of my favorite lists from the green folder is a collection of *actual statements* made on insurance forms by people who had been in car accidents—more evidence that we don't have to go too far to find humor.

—Coming home, I drove into the wrong house and collided with a tree I didn't have.

—The guy was all over the road: I had to swerve a number of times before I finally hit him.

—I pulled away from the side of the road, glanced at my mother-in-law, and headed over the embankment.

—In my attempt to kill a fly, I drove into a telephone pole.

—I had been driving my car for forty years when I fell asleep at the wheel and had an accident.

—The pedestrian had no idea which direction to go, so I ran over him.

—The telephone pole was approaching fast. I was attempting to swerve out of its path when it struck my front end.

Perhaps the funniest things I've seen though, however, were some actual faux paus from church bulletins. In our church one Sunday, the confessional prayer in the bulletin should have read, "Forgive us, O Lord, in our private prayers." But due to a small typographical slip it appeared, "Forgive us, O Lord, in our primate prayers." (Actually, it made me feel a little more at home.)

The following slips actually appeared in church bulletins around the country.

—This afternoon there will be a meeting in the north and south ends of the church and children will be christened at both ends.

—Tuesday at 7 p.m. there will be an invitation to an ice-cream social. All ladies giving milk, please come early.

—Wednesday, the Ladies Literary Society will meet and

Mrs. Lacey will sing, "Put Me in My Little Bed," accompanied by the Reverend.

—This Sunday being Easter, we will ask Mrs. Daley to come forward and lay an egg on the altar.

I hope something in one of those lists brought slight tears of laughter to your eyes. If any were offensive to you, I sincerely apologize, but they were only meant to bring to your life and mine a little more laughter. Personally, I believe it is far more immoral to go through life and not enjoy it than to be tickled by the humor that is all around us!

## Life Is Difficult

Scott Peck opens his brilliant best-seller, *The Road Less Traveled,* with this statement: "Life is difficult." He continues:

> This is a great truth, one of the greatest truths. It is a great truth because once we truly see this truth, we transcend it. Once we truly know that life is difficult—once we truly understand and accept it—then life is no longer difficult. Because once it has been accepted, the fact that life is difficult no longer matters.
>
> Most do not fully see this truth that life is difficult. Instead they moan more or less incessantly, noisily or subtly, about the enormity of their problems, their burdens, and their difficulties as if life were generally easy, as if life *should* be easy. They voice their belief, noisily or subtly, that their difficulties represent a unique kind of affliction that should not be and that has somehow been especially visited upon them, or else upon their families, their tribe, their class, their nation, their race or even their species, and not upon others. I know about this moaning because I have done my share.[8]
>
> SCOTT PECK

One of the most common and naive sentences in the English language is perhaps the following: "If I can just get through this problem, then everything will be all right." There comes a time, and it may well be the birth of maturity, when we realize that once we get through our present problem there will be another one, slightly larger and a little more intense, waiting to take its place.

Problems are the litmus paper of the human story. How we respond to them may well be a measure of our health. All of us feel overwhelmed at some time or another. But problems in and of themselves are not necessarily bad. In fact, the root of the word *problem* means "to throw or to drive forward." A life without problems would be meaningless and empty. The difficulty is that for most of us our problems are often nameless, routinely dull and, at times, apparently unsolvable.

Most of the problems that wait for us are homely and familiar if still uncomfortable to deal with or to acknowledge. It is not, in other words, the dramatic life that is crowded with difficulties. You don't have to have Romanoff bad luck or be born under a surly star in order to discover your share of difficulties. . . . We don't really get through life by solving problems in a final way but by responding more adequately as we move along.
. . .

Living with everyday problems demands a readiness to vote in favor of life and of the pains and joys that go with it. It involves an acceptance of ourselves as we are and a willingness to grow into the best version of our personality that is possible. The values that are lasting will be tapped in our passage through life: the question of whether we can believe or hope or touch people with love. These will, in a very real sense, provide the center of gravity and the strength that we need in order to make our journey by the route that is best for us. The trip becomes increasingly joyful as we give ourselves wholeheartedly to it. The biggest problem is that simple everyday one of being human. We solve it only bit by bit in the process of living itself.[9]

EUGENE KENNEDY

The Bible is certainly not oblivious to difficulty. But it is critical that we begin to understand Scripture's message that difficulty and joy are not exclusive entities, but mutual friends.

Consider it pure joy, my brothers, whenever you face trials of many kinds, because you know that the testing of your faith develops perseverance. Perseverance must finish its work so that you may be mature and complete, not lacking anything.

JAMES 1:2-4

Most of the Psalms were born in difficulty. Most of the Epistles were written in prisons. Most of the greatest thoughts of the greatest thinkers of all time had to pass through the fire. Bunyan wrote *Pilgrim's Progress* from jail. Florence Nightingale, too ill to move from her bed, reorganized the hospitals of England. Semiparalyzed and under the constant menace of apoplexy, Pasteur was tireless in his attack on disease. During the greater part of his life, American historian Francis Parkman suffered so acutely that he could not work for more than five minutes at a time. His eyesight was so wretched that he could scrawl only a few gigantic words on a manuscript, yet he contrived to write twenty magnificent volumes of history. Sometimes it seems that when God is about to make preeminent use of a man, he puts him through the fire.[10]

Many people live as though they regret God's incred-

87

ible invitation to life. Avoiding pain becomes their chief occupation. And few of them realize that avoidance of difficulty only produces more pain in the long run.

Certain religious circles today would have us believe that the ideal spiritual life is one where problems are instantaneously solved and miracles never cease. They insist that to be saved means to be safe and opens one up to a charmed life in which anyone who does not prosper and live affluently is not living fully in the Spirit.

Perhaps this has been true for some people. It has not been my experience. And according to my limited observations, it does not seem to be biblical. The Bible, above all else, seems to be a book of reality. And reality has the mark of difficulty.

On one side is the message of hope. The Scriptures say that the righteous shall flourish like the palm tree— but we need to remember that palm trees don't grow in beautiful forests, but in the desert. We are called to bear fruit—but we must recognize that the fruit tree grows in valleys, not on mountaintops.

The heroes of this book are not knights in shining armor nor persons born with golden tongues nor giants lumpy with great muscles. They are just people who discovered something in God and in themselves which was a mixture of the majestic and the ordinary, the divine and the human. When their circumstances seemed to overwhelm them, they had the ability to rise to the occasion and give the glory to God.

The Bible is first-hand story of goose bump courage in very ordinary people—who were invaded by the living God. And amidst all the difficulties of modern day living, the story continues today. The great ones today are ordinary folk who have opened their lives up to a new dimension and who do not simply tolerate difficulties, but lean into them.

Life is difficult. There is no way to get around it. We need to remind ourselves of it each day. Hence, it requires that we have something or Someone within us to encounter the mishaps and transcend them.

I simply believe that there is a mystery of the ordinary, that the commonplace is full of wonder, and that this life that we call Christian is different from what we think it is. It is infinitely more subtle, more powerful, more dangerous, more magnificent, more exciting, more humorous, more delicious, more adventurous, more involved, and more troublesome than most of us think. Through Christ each of us is capable of an almost unbounded courage of compassion, and that to live fully this life that God has given us, no matter what circumstances may be, can be a rare and ennobling experience.

I believe that pain and suffering can either be a prison or a prism. The tests of life are not to break us but to make us. We're called not to flinch from real trouble, for the greater part of life occurs in the inner man.

> So do not throw away your confidence; it will be richly rewarded. "My righteous one will live by faith, and if he shrinks back, I will not be pleased with him."
>
> HEBREWS 10:35, 38

St. Paul wrote an incredible epistle of freedom to the people of Galatia. In his next to last sentence, he says, "Let no one interfere with me after this. I carry on my scarred body the marks of Jesus" (Galatians 6:17, Phillips). He didn't *think* the truth would set him free.

He didn't *believe* the truth would set him free. He *knew* the truth would set him free. He had an eyeball-to-eyeball experience with the risen Christ and discovered that the freedom he was called to was not painless, easy, nor without difficulty. But it was real. Many of us have had the same experience.

A few years ago, I read the story of a young man who was a quadriplegic and yet affirmed life with an immense sense of joy. He radiated a quality of life to all those who knew him. When asked what was his secret he said, "Even the mere fact of dressing is such an inordinate difficulty that it is almost impossible for me. When life becomes this difficult, you know darn well I'm going to make sure that it's *quality.*"

In 1962 research scientists Victor and Mildred Goertzel published the provocative and revealing *Cradles of Eminence.* Its purpose was to study 413 "famous and exceptionally gifted people" and learn what produced such lives. The patterns which emerged from the very beginning of the study were startling. For example, approximately eighty percent of the later famous children loathed school. Seven out of ten eminent persons came from homes which in no way could be considered warm or peaceful. Rather they were homes riddled with traumas such as missing or argumentative parents, poverty, and physical handicaps. Almost every conceivable handicap had been successfully overcome by some eminent person. The book provided some revealing insights into the roots of people who were later to be called "great." Virtually all of them had overcome severe difficulties in order to become the people they were called to be.

Perhaps God gives us difficulties in order to give us the opportunity to know who we really are and who we really can be. We live in a world that is sometimes constipated by its own superficiality. But life's difficulties are even a privilege, in that they allow us or force us to break through the superficiality to the deeper life within.

# The Advantages of Disadvantages

*Make me to hear joy and gladness,*
*Let the bones which Thou hast broken rejoice.*

PSALM 51:8, NASB

*If I am in sickness,*
*my sickness may serve Him;*
*If I am in sorrow,*
*my sorrow may serve Him.*
*He does nothing in vain,*
*He knows what He is about.*

JOHN HENRY NEWMAN

*Satisfy us in the morning with your unfailing love,*
*that we may sing for joy and be glad all our days.*
*Make us glad for as many days as you have afflicted us,*
*for as many years as we have seen trouble.*

PSALM 90:14-16

*The only cure for suffering is to face it head on, grasp it*
*around the neck, and use it.*

MARY CRAIG

THE BIG DREAM IN OUR SOCIETY is that if we work hard enough, we will eventually be able to experience a life without limitations or difficulties. It is also one of the biggest sources of friction in our society, creating disappointment, unnecessary suffering, and missed opportunities to live a full life. Some people spend their entire life waiting for that which will never, and can never, happen.

Limitations are not necessarily negative. In fact, I'm beginning to believe that they can give life definition, clarity, and *freedom*. We are called to a freedom *of* and *in* limitations—not *from*. Unrestricted water is a swamp—because it lacks restriction, it also lacks depth.

The conclusion we arrive at all depends upon how we look at our limitations. Consider this late-night phone call I received one night. The voice on the other end inquired with great enthusiasm: "What does it mean for a horse to be handicapped!"

She hadn't identified herself, but I knew who it was. Leigh is a very special friend, and we've been through much together. She not only suffers from severe cerebral palsy, but has faced other, sometimes even more severe, difficulties—like losing her family at an age too young. Her feistiness and tenacity are not only her hallmarks, but are a contagious influence on us all.

I responded to her question, "Well, Leigh, I'm not exactly into horse racing, but as far as I understand, they usually handicap the strongest horse by adding a little extra weight. It's done in order to make the race more fair."

"Yeah, I know!"

Then she asked: "What does it mean if you handicap a golfer?"

"Well, Leigh—again, I'm not really sure. But as far as

I understand the rules, they handicap the best in order to make the game more exciting. The better the golfer, the larger his handicap.

"Yeah, I know. And what does it mean when a bowler is handicapped?"

After we explored a number of sports, always reaching the same conclusion, there was a rather long pause. Then she said, with bold simplicity: *"That's it!"*

"That's what, Leigh?" I replied, not understanding.

*"That's it!* That's why God gave me such a big handicap . . . *because I'm so special!"*

It was one of the finest statements for tenacious dignity in spite of circumstances that I have ever heard.

Leigh is a fighter, special beyond description. And because of that, this Jesus is going to continue to "win in the end" in her life. We need more like her. As Winston Churchill put it:

> Success is never final; Failure is never fatal; It is Courage that counts.

## Acceptance

A certain measure of our maturity lies in the fuller dimensions of acceptance, of allowing the transitions that are difficult but necessary to take place.

Victor Frankl, in his classic *Man's Search for Meaning,* shares the incredible tragedies that he had to go through when thrown into a Nazi concentration camp where he was stripped of everything. He lost his friends, his life work, the manuscripts he was working on, and even his family. At one point he reached a place so low that he said they had literally taken everything in his life except one thing: the attitude with which he chose to respond to the situation.

This became a vital and significant turning point in his life, and it was from this discovery that he developed the concept of logo therapy—in essence the ability to find meaning through every event in life, even those most difficult.

One of the greatest tragedies of our modern civilization is that you and I can live a trivial life and get away with it. One of the great advantages of pain and suffering is that it forces us to break through our superficial crusts to discover life on a deeper and more meaningful level.

I recently found a simple but surprising sentence by St. Paul in II Corinthians 10:7, "You are looking only on the surface of things." Pain forces you to look below the surface. The tragedy is that many of us never have the courage to choose to do that. Hence we waste much of our life in bitterness and complaint, always looking for something else, never realizing that perhaps God has already given us sufficient grace to discover all of what we are looking for in the midst of our own circumstances.

St. Thomas Aquinas told of a man who heard about a very special ox and determined to have it for his own. He traveled all over the world. He spent his entire fortune. He gave his whole life to the search for this ox. At last, just moments before he died, he realized *he had been riding it all the time.*

I had never told my folks that parable of the ox, but one day there arrived at my home a package bearing a familiar return address. My bargain-hunting mom, who loves to shop at thrift stores, had been habitually sending me wood carvings from all her favorite shops. It's true that I have a special place in my heart for wood carvings, but some of these weren't exactly the kind you find displayed at the county fair. Quite a few really fit the image of a bargain! So with something less than enthusiasm, I opened the latest. And inside I found something I will treasure for the rest of my life: an exquisite, almost unbelievable carving of a man riding an ox.

Mom had no way of knowing the significance that carving would have for me, but the man riding the ox has been sitting on my dresser ever since. It's the first thing I see in the morning and the last thing I see as I go to bed—a strong reminder that God has already given me all that I'm looking for.

I'm convinced that most of us, even in our most difficult situations, have everything we are looking for—if we would but choose to accept it and embrace it. Most of us already are in the place where God wants us to be—if we were but willing to deepen our roots, increase our courage, and expand our vision and hope.

## Transformation

Another advantage of disadvantages is that we have the opportunity to be transformed by our suffering. To be pushed. Pulled. Moved in one direction or another. Pain and suffering produce a fork in the road. It is not possible to remain unchanged. To let others or circumstances dictate your future is to have chosen. To allow the pain to corrode your spirit is to have chosen. And to be transformed into the image of Christ by these difficult and trying circumstances is to have chosen.

> Jesus did not come to explain away suffering or remove it. He came to fill it with his Presence.
>
> PAUL CLAUDEL

Hebrews 5:8 surprises us by saying, "Although

[Jesus] was a son, he learned obedience from what he suffered." If even the Master had to go through suffering to learn obedience, why should it be any less necessary for us?

Romans 5:3-5 offers incredible encouragement in the midst of our trials. "We also rejoice in our sufferings, because we know that suffering produces perseverance; perseverance, character; and character, hope. And hope does not disappoint us, because God has poured out his love into our hearts by the Holy Spirit, whom he has given us." This theme is repeated again and again throughout the New Testament.

I believe the purpose of trials is to help us truly discover, at a level we can only know by painful experience, the real meaning of JOY. This joy then sets us free for a new and more powerful kind of service. And this service helps us to understand, perhaps as we would never have been able to otherwise, what it really means to know God.

## Seeing Differently

Years ago I read a remarkable story that took place in a burn ward. The woman who wrote it, Mary Moore, had slipped in the shower one night, hitting the hot water handle on the way down and turning her pleasant shower into a scalding, terrifying experience. Much of her body was covered with third-degree burns.

Perhaps no pain is as excruciating as that of being burned, and no process more traumatic than that of having to have skin grafted back onto the body. But in the midst of her trauma she met a man who introduced himself simply as Sarge. It was obvious by looking at him that his burns were far worse than hers, and she later heard stories of the incredibly painful things he had undergone just to survive. And yet this man was continually at her bedside, offering her a cup of coffee or some juice, asking if he could be of service. She discovered that he did this with many patients on the ward. Although his pain was probably the worst, he had somehow found within himself the ability to transcend it and serve others.

His spirit was contagious. He brought hope and life and love to a place whose middle name was tragedy. She was amazed at his bouyant spirit and depth of compassion. More than anything, he seemed to see the world differently because of the pain he knew by experience. Lives were not only touched and changed, but some were perhaps even saved by this man's remarkable ability to see differently and care enough to be involved.

She had been raised in the south, brought up on the importance of manners and etiquette. Yet what he conveyed was more than kindness; it was genuine compassion.

One evening they chatted at length. He said with excitement that after a few more operations he would be able to go back to his family, whom he loved so deeply. He described how wonderful his children were and how proud he was of his wife, for she had even graduated from college. Naturally the writer inquired as to which college, and when he told her she was stunned.

"Sarge, that's a black college. Your wife isn't black, is she?"

He was quiet for a long moment and then said, "Yes, ma'am. What color did you think I was?"[1]

Their shared pain allowed them to transcend a

barrier which would have otherwise been imposed. Because of a great disadvantage, she had the privilege of meeting a man who would teach her how to see the world through different eyes.

We live in a society that looks only on the surfaces. But pain, if allowed, produces an identification with the suffering of others, and even with Christ, that we could not experience in any other way. One is allowed to see dignity in the midst of human struggle and see beyond the false barriers that are oftentimes imposed between human beings. If our maturity grows, perhaps we even learn to see Christ in each other and even in ourselves.

In the inevitable ache of the world, I never cease to be amazed by the use of first person singular in Matthew 25 when our Lord said, "I was hungry and you fed me. I was thirsty and you gave me something to drink. I was cold and you came to me with a blanket. I was alone and you came and visited me."

## Gratitude, Wonder, and Appreciation

If we are but willing to learn, our disadvantages can renew a deeper appreciation for the simple things in life. I remember one day visiting with Joni Eareckson Tada, the gifted author/artist/singer who has been a quadriplegic since a diving accident at age seventeen. It was one of those days when my pain level was excruciatingly high, almost intolerable. At times I had difficulty just focusing on our conversation. The day seemed incredibly long.

When I got home I was so worn out that I collapsed at the kitchen table and indulged in a bout of self-pity. As hard as it is to admit, it even crossed my mind that Joni was better off than I am, in that she feels no pain.

Suddenly my younger son, Joshua, came running into the room and jumped into my arms. As I hugged him, I had a stunned and embarrassed realization: Joni, who had been so bouyant and cheerful all day, would never be able to experience giving such a hug. Perhaps for the first time in my life, I realized that being able to give my son a hug was a *gift* and not a right.

That evening I began to look at my pain from the other end of the tunnel. I realized again that I was blessed with a continual reminder that all of life is a gift and even the simplest acts and events are meant to be treasured.

I know that I'm a slow learner, but my appetite for wonder has never been greater. My appreciation for so-called ordinary things has never been richer.

Perhaps I could have learned these things otherwise, but I think not. In my more honest moments, I realize that some things I thought I just had to endure were really hidden blessings meant to teach me how special life itself is.

## The Freedom of Limitations: Focus

Jeanette Harvey has spent her life in a wheelchair. She says the big failure of many people is our tendency to look at the limitations of being disabled, rather than the assets. She is now a very successful career woman, but it has not been achieved without a fight, without pain, or without suffering from the double distinction of being disabled and female.

Among the "assets that result from disability" Jeanette names the limitation of choice, which makes it easier to focus all one's energy on the possible instead of diluting and scattering it. Both a light bulb and a laser beam are essentially light energy, but while we hold our hands in front of a light bulb without danger of being burned, there are laser beams that can burn through eighteen inches of solid steel. The difference is a matter of focus.

In a world that inundates us with choices, one can become disoriented and almost overwhelmed by too many options. Life can become thinned out by trying to do too many things. One of the advantages of disadvantages is the privilege of being forced to see that which is closer, that which is simple, that which has been given to you. Life must have limitations in order to have depth.

Caught once in a terrible fog, I realized that I couldn't see anything in the distance. So I took advantage of the situation, slowed down, and relished the beauty that was close at hand. How few people there are who know how to participate passionately in a larger *now* that is already clothed with timelessness. I have friends who have learned how to listen to a single day in their life, a single moment, a single event with almost ferocious intensity, passion, and joy, in spite—or is it because of?—their limitations.

What we have traditionally perceived as limitations are sometimes the lens which can bring our life into deeper and finer focus.

## A Different Kind of Strength

. . . There was given me a thorn in my flesh . . . to torment me. Three times I pleaded with the Lord to take it away from me. But he said to me, "My grace is sufficient for you, for my power is made perfect in weakness." Therefore I will boast all the more gladly about my weaknesses, so that Christ's power may rest on me. That is why, for Christ's sake, I delight in weakness-

es, in insults, in hardships, in persecutions, in difficulties. For when I am weak, then I am strong.

II CORINTHIANS 12:8-10

Time and time again, throughout both the Old and
the New Testament, God expresses his desire to give us
*his* genuine strength and power. Paul reminds us that
one of the greatest limiting factors to receiving that
power is our temptation to rely on our own strength.

Most of my life my energy and strength has been
based on talent, effort, pushing and striving. I spent
much if not most of my Christian life thinking about
what I could do for Jesus, rather that what he could do
in me. Perhaps it is by God's grace that I'm no longer
able to do all those things but must learn a new kind of
receptivity, a new kind of residing power, another kind
of strength from a source which is not my own. In
letting go—because I had to—I've discovered a more
permanent kind of eternal peace and power.

> For this reason I kneel before the Father . . . [and]
> pray that out of his glorious riches he may strengthen
> you with power through his Spirit in your inner being,
> so that Christ may dwell in your hearts through faith.
> And I pray that you, being rooted and established in
> love, may have power . . . to grasp how wide and long
> and high and deep is the love of Christ, and to know
> this love that surpasses knowledge—that you may be
> filled to the measure of all the fullness of God.
>
> Now to him who is able to do immeasurably more
> than all we ask or imagine, according to his power that
> is at work within us, to him be glory . . . for ever and
> ever!
>
> EPHESIANS 3:14-21

That passage is perhaps one of my favorites, for it

reminds me of how much God wants to give us. It has been said that it is not so much our *ability* that counts as our *availability*. In Ephesians 1:19, 20, Paul says, "How tremendous is the power available to us who believe in God. That power is the same divine energy which was demonstrated in Christ when He raised Him from the dead and gave Him a place of supreme honor in Heaven." We have available to us the veritable Easter power, but we can live out our whole Christian lives blindfolded to it—because we've never *really* had to depend on his power and his power alone.

## Choice

Paul Tournier says that perhaps the most powerful and unused gift from God is choice. For me a big step in maturity was letting go of the fantasy of some magical cure and beginning to understand that pain can either integrate or disintegrate me. The choice is up to me.

Pain is teaching me how to choose more forcefully, more boldly. I'm learning how to say no with more aggressiveness, sometimes because I simply have to. I'm learning how to say yes with more honesty and openness because my life has become more vulnerable.

The root of the word *decide* means "to cut." Perhaps one of the advantages of disadvantages is the fact that we have to cut. We have to make choices which we didn't have to at earlier stages in our life.

> Pain is part of the process. . . . From the shedding of blood that initiates birth to the last gasp of astonishment in the face of death, we are encircled in suffering. The biography of a human being is also a history of anguish. The way one reacts to the suffering of life matters

more, in creative and human terms, than the suffering itself. We become the people we are through the disadvantages and conflicts we prefer to more comfortable alternatives.[2]

ANTHONY T. PABOVANO

In the 1952 Olympics a young Hungarian boy looked down his pistol barrel and split the bull's-eye again and again—he just couldn't miss. With that perfect right hand and eye coordination, he won a gold medal. Six months later he lost his right arm. But in Melbourne four years later he came back and split the bull's-eye again and again, winning his second gold medal with his left hand. He chose not to be limited by his limitations.

Necessity is the author of change. Sometimes we only learn because we have to. Our level of joy (and therefore strength and healing) is directly proportionate to our level of acceptance. Our attitude is the key. Slowly I'm learning how to love even the dents in my life and embrace even the ambiguities and difficulties.

## Holy and Crazy and Wonderful Grace

We know sorrow, yet our joy is inextinguishable.

II CORINTHIANS 6:10

GRACE. Perhaps no one ever completely understands it. Few of us wholly recognize the work of grace in our lives—yet God wants more than anything for us to experience it with as much fullness as we can handle.

Why do so many miss it? I think it's for a number of reasons. One, as mentioned earlier, is that we get stuck in the surface of life. We get caught up with *doing,* to the exclusion of the *being* element of our faith.

105

A second reason, as indicated, is our insistence on self-sufficiency—an apparently harmless tendency which detours us from a greater sense of completeness than we would ever imagine.

A third, that I would like to suggest again, is our avoidance of pain, which inadvertently closes the door to the life in grace that we are seeking at the deepest levels. A clenched fist cannot receive. Folded arms cannot embrace. Our fear of pain blocks our ability to hear God at the deepest levels. Interestingly enough, the word obedience comes from the root *obadare* which means "to listen."

I recently discovered that there are 365 "fear nots" in the Bible. Could it be that it is to remind us *daily* that we need not fear the difficulties that all of us eventually have to face?

One of my favorites is found in Isaiah 43. God begins by saying boldly: "FEAR NOT, for I have redeemed you; I HAVE CALLED YOU BY NAME, YOU ARE MINE."

That is the essential reason why we need not fear. Then he continues:

When you pass *through* the waters,
    I will be with you. And when you pass *through* the rivers,
    they will not sweep over you.
When [*not if*] you walk *through* the fire,
    you will not be burned;
    the flames will not set you ablaze.
Since you are precious and honored in my sight
    and because I love you. . . .
    Do not be afraid, for I am with you.

ISAIAH 43:2, 4, 5

I purposely emphasized the word *through* because I

106

think it is critical. We must accept and go *through* our difficulties in order to find the kind of peace, joy, endurance, steadfastness, and indefatigable hope that God wants for us in our journey to become more like his Son. His steadfast promise is his presence *in the midst* of going *through.*

One of our central problems—most assuredly mine— is that I'd just as soon go around. I prefer detours to the rough road of through-ness. When given the opportunity, my tendency is to avoid difficulty rather than facing it squarely.

Consider the following poem:

Feeling blue?
Buy some clothes.
Feeling lonely?
Turn on the radio.
Feeling despondent?
Read a funny book.
Feeling bored?
Watch TV.
Feeling empty?
Eat a sundae.
Feeling worthless?
Clean the house.
Feeling sad?
Tell a joke.
Ain't this modern age wonderful?
You don't gotta feel nothin',
There's a substitute for everythin'!

God have mercy on us![3]

LOIS A. CHENEY

Grace is the central invitation to life, and the final word. It's the beckoning nudge and the overwhelming, undeserved mercy which urges us to change and grow, and then gives us the power to pull it off.

The trouble with steeling yourself against the harshness of reality is that the same steel that secures your life against being destroyed secures your life also against being opened up and transformed by the holy power that life itself comes from. You can survive on your own. You can grow strong on your own. You can even prevail on your own. But you cannot become human on your own. Surely that is why, in Jesus' sad joke, the rich man has as hard a time getting into Paradise as that camel through the needle's eye because with his credit card in his pocket, the rich man is so effective at getting for himself everything he needs that he does not see that what he needs more than anything else in the world can be had only as a gift.[4]

FREDERICK BUECHNER

Grace: a worn-out and tired word that people tend to avoid or, worse yet, bounce around flippantly. But the reality is rich, vivid, powerful. Grace: that overexposed and underexperienced gift from beyond, to help us struggle through the dailyness of our time, and perhaps lighten our step and point the way. A glimpse, not just of what life can be, but of what life really is. Grace: a gentle wedge that separates the shadows amidst our crowded and exhausting days. Grace: it is not of reason, but experience—this holy, wonderful, wild, and crazy-beyond-us-yet-within-us life of God.

We can't possess it but, paradoxically, it possesses us. When we begin to let go, to release our brakes, we can taste its transcendence, even though we can't own it and, oftentimes, cannot fully understand it.

What but grace could "turn your sorrow into . . . a joy that no one can take from you." (John 16:20, 22)

Our limitations can become the very invitation to discover fully the dimensions of grace, the improbable path to God's otherwise hidden blessing. God does his good work within us and wants to continue to expand it, not because of who we are, but because of who he is.

That which appears to us to be limitation can actually become our unexpected advantage and asset. As we're forced to our knees once again, we discover the holy and wonder-full gift of life.

# PART THREE

# THE JOURNEY CONTINUES

*In the
midst of winter.
I finally discovered within me
an invincible summer.*

*Albert Camus*

# Peace
# Inside the Pain

*A bird doesn't sing because he has an answer—he sings because he has a song.*

JOAN ANGLUND

*We shall not cease from exploration and the end of all our exploring will be to arrive where we started and know the place for the first time.*

T. S. ELIOT

*Just to be is a blessing*
*Just to live is holy.*

ABRAHAM HESCHEL

WILLIAM STAFFORD WAS ONCE ASKED in an interview, "When did you decide to become a poet?" He responded that the question was put wrongly: "Everyone is born a poet—a person discovering the way words sound and work, caring and delighting in words. I just kept on doing what everyone starts out doing. The real question is why did other people stop?"[1]

We all need to discover and keep rediscovering the poetry of our own existence. All of our lives are like patchwork quilts. How dull and dreary they would be without darker patches to contrast with the lighter ones. Many of us have never realized how dreary and lifeless our existence would be without problems and difficulties. Part of the blessing of the human journey is that we are, in fact, human, and therefore wonderfully complex and changing constantly.

The longer I live the more appreciative I become of the fact that life is not tidy and predictable. But it is filled with all the emotions that we can handle—and sometimes even more. I'm grateful that we never know who we will become—and that's why it's called a journey.

In *Oh God, Book II,* George Burns, playing the part of God, is asked by a tiny girl why bad things happen. Burns thoughtfully considers her question and then replies. "That's the way the system works. . . . Have you ever seen an up, without a down? A front, without a back? A top, without a bottom? You can't have one without the other. I discovered that if I take away sad, then I take away happy, too. They go together." Then, with a wry smile, he adds, "If somebody has a better idea, I hope they put it in the suggestion box."

*Oh God, Book II* was never meant to be a theological film. But even in the midst of its comedy, it can remind us that the many sides of life are meant to fit together.

Ten years is a long time. I suppose that even if nothing had happened, I would still be different. But something did happen along the way, perhaps more by God's grace than by my efforts. So in many ways, I now begin a new season and I shall be different. I *am* different. I've learned some important things and, as Michelangelo said at the peak of his career, "still I am learning."

I am learning that there is a center within all of us where truth abides in fullness—and that it can be discovered and, even more importantly, it can be experienced. I'm learning that it's worth all the pain to find it. And that wherever possible, we're meant to share it. I am learning that each moment of life is in itself a sacred privilege. Life's moments are complete in themselves. Part of the joy is discovering that; the better part is participating in it.

A friend of mine mixed up his words one day and said, "All we have is the past, the pleasant, and the future." We thought it was even a better way to echo a truth that all too many of us miss. Few Christians recognize how radical their posture in the world truly is. Their past is absolutely forgiven and their future is absolutely certain, so that, more than any other body of people on the face of the earth, they are free to live in the "pleasant tense."

The signature of pain has left a mark on all of our faces. Although there is much desperate pain in the world, there is also another kind of pain.

> This is the suffering of a healthy person, as undramatic as it is inevitable, as commonplace as it is uncomforted. It is the pain with a thousand private faces, the pain that comes from just being human. No man is inoculated against the ache of his struggle to become himself as a human being and a child of God.[2]
>
> EUGENE KENNEDY

Suffering, in fact, is guaranteed for anyone who takes on the task of living. They will suffer, but they will also find fullness of life and a personal experience of the Spirit's presence.

\*     \*     \*

*Summer, 1982*
*For years I've managed to have enough creative incompetence*
*to need massive doses of God's mercy. My incompetence in my*
*marriage hasn't always been creative, but it has certainly led to*
*the need for extra doses of God's mercy—or more.*

\*     \*     \*

People sometimes ask what impact the accident has had on my family. It has been extensive. Statistics show that trauma of any sort will have a major influence on a family's survival. It took me years to understand that my pain was often worse on my family and my friends than it was on me. For a long period of time, my selfish preoccupation simply blinded me to that fact.

There were other contributing factors, I'm sure, but at the end of 1982, our beautiful marriage began to fall apart. It was not to recover till over a year later. That was the longest year of my life. When people ask which is worse, emotional pain or physical pain, I find the answer simple. Emotional pain far outweighs the other. But during that year I discovered grace firsthand at levels I had never known before.

I remember a call that year from a dear Episcopal friend. He said, "You evangelicals still all believe that God's grace and mercy depend on the beauty and the faithfulness of the believer. They don't." He reminded me of one of the greatest truths, so easy to forget— God's mercy depends on his character, not on ours.

Some people reading this book will say, "I can't identify. Your pain has been different than mine." Perhaps. But during that year I discovered that the spectrum of pain is wider and deeper than I thought.

By God's grace Pam and I were able to put the pieces back together. And after over a year of separation, we now enjoy a relationship far beyond anything we'd ever known. But I know that I am in a blessed minority.

Many of you reading this have experienced situations that did not make it or remain still unresolved. I simply invite you to remember the promise, "Goodness and mercy unfailing, these will follow me all the days of my life." The hound of heaven will pursue us recklessly until he can overwhelm us with his mercy, his love, and his goodness.

## Dancin' Lessons

In another section I dared to indicate that there are, in fact, assets to disability if we have the courage to look at them as such. But there are also serious liabilities, and it is important to recognize these as well, so we can anticipate the difficulties and learn proper mechanisms for coping with them. Pain has many by-products that can sneak up on us if we're not aware. How *do* we "keep on dancin'" in the midst of these?

## FATIGUE

People often say to me, "How difficult it must be to be in pain all the time." I usually reply that I have gotten somewhat used to the pain, but the thing that bothers me more is its constant companion, fatigue.

The word *exhaust* comes from a Latin word meaning "to draw out of." Perhaps one of my greatest frustrations is that feeling of emptiness, of being drained of all natural resources, of being "used up" before my time.

One of the best things we can do for those in pain is to encourage them to slow down, focus more on being than doing, and adjust to a more limited energy span.

When we're suffering, whether from chronic pain or deep sorrow, we must remember to focus more on what we *can* do than what we cannot, more on the privilege of being alive than on the deprivation of energy. We need to monitor rest very carefully. Learn how to nap or take ten- to fifteen-minute breaks where you can relax your body totally and give it rest.

## SELF-PREOCCUPATION

Next to the genuine fatigue of pain, possibly the most energy-depriving thing I know is self-pity. I know from firsthand experience that it is one of the greatest wastes of my time and emotions, yet I confess my vulnerability to it.

My greatest need at these times is for people who will listen to me compassionately, but then firmly and gently encourage me out of such dreadful behavior. It is important that people don't join me in my self-pity party, but love me into remembering what I can do and must do.

One definition of a coward is simply "someone who makes a lot of excuses." Most of us have enough excuses to last a lifetime. The sooner we let go of them and get on with living, the better off we are.

Though pain is both a personal and private journey, it inevitably affects the lives of those closest to us and imposes limitations on them as well. Pain is a shared experience, whether we want it to be or not.

I have some very special and close friends, including my wife, who are invaluable in helping me maintain a proper perspective. One day Pam sent me a quote that said, "I love you too much to let you be less than the best." It's this kind of hard-nosed agape that enables us to continue our quest, in spite of the obstacles and feelings that get in our way.

## GUILT

I find that I can feel guilty about most anything these days—being overweight, being overtired, being distracted by pain, not being able to perform as I used to. It's an ongoing battle. Perhaps one of the best things I've ever read about guilt was this simple statement: "No one benefits from your guilt." This simple fact, more than any other, has forced me to let go of some of the guilt that I seem to want to carry around.

My guilt, your guilt, benefits no one. Although it's a natural phenomenon, and a common by-product of pain, we need to do anything we can to let go of it. We are who we are. The past is just that—poof. We can choose freedom.

> For freedom Christ has set us free. Stand fast, therefore, and do not submit again to a yoke of slavery.
> GALATIANS 5:1

## DEPRESSION

Recently I was asked an unusual and provocative question: Do you like your body? It came on one of those days when I felt somewhere to the left of awful.

"I used to," I replied. I could remember days when I had unbounded energy and could do almost anything physically. I never struggled with how I looked or how I felt. I once ran fifty miles nonstop, just to see if I could do it.

I've gone through a lot of physical and mental changes in the past ten years. Sometimes it's difficult to

119

accept my situation. Sometimes it's difficult to accept myself. The result can be depression—that insidious dull grey feeling that life has lost its flavor.

Depression is an extension of both guilt and anger turned inward. If you struggle with depression you need to know: 1) you're normal, 2) it's an inevitable by-product of what you've experienced, and 3) it doesn't last forever.

If your depression is serious enough to be a strong impediment in your life, I'd suggest that you talk to someone about it. Sometimes it helps greatly to be able to talk openly and honestly and vent your frustrations. Dialogue has a phenomenal ability to clarify issues.

If your depression continues, you might want to consider counseling. I believe in it strongly. Often a professionally trained counselor can penetrate the core of the problem and help you turn the corner. Your counselor may recommend consulting a doctor. Many people don't realize that our body chemistry changes amidst depression, and the chemical imbalances are often a big part of why the depression continues.

A typical response of someone suffering is to stop exercising. But exercise, especially of large muscle groups produces chemicals that fight depression and low spirits. Believe it or not, exercise may be one of the most important things that we can do in the midst of pain or sorrow or grief. Walking, cycling, jogging, or other aerobic exercise changes not only the chemicals in our bodies but our very attitudes. It is one of the best known forms of relaxation ever to be discovered by man.

(By the way, after giving it more thought, I changed my response to the friend who asked how I felt about my body. My revised conclusion: "You bet I like my body. Not only is it the only one I'll ever have, but I can't believe it's still ticking after all the abuse I've given it.")

## CONFUSION/INDECISION

"At this time I want you to know that my maybe is definite!" Whether your pain is physical, emotional, mental, or spiritual, you are under added *stress.* This can cause indecisiveness and confusion (which can then cause guilt—and the cycle continues). Likewise, if you're struggling with depression, one of its major and quite natural symptoms is confused thinking.

Sometimes the pieces of the puzzle need to be separated and spread around before they can be put together in a new way.

In my own life, what has helped the most are:
1) having someone I can share with at a very open and honest level.
2) giving myself the gift of privacy and stillness to think things through. It can be as simple as taking yourself to dinner once every couple weeks, or it can mean blocking out a few days away for a period of solitude. (Local missions or monasteries are more available for this purpose than most of us realize.)
3) beginning the day with a brief period of stillness. Spending time in God's Word does amazing things to clarify our direction.

### Earthen Vessels

As I learn new levels of giving over my situation to the Lord, I realize that it not only lessens my pain but increases my ability to be joyful in the midst of the circumstances.

Acceptance means that I accept the process. It has

been said that Jesus came not to take away suffering, but to help us make our suffering more like his and to give it meaning.

Acceptance means to stop avoiding and start leaning into my particular situation. Despite our inability to control circumstances, we are given the gift of being free to respond to our situation in our own way, creatively or destructively.

Acceptance means that I allow the process to transform me into the image of God's Son. It means that I'm willing to let go of who I think I ought to be, and become who God wants me to be.

The more we fight our pain and sorrow, the more tense we become and the more the pain is amplified. When we stop grasping for immediate solutions, relax into the present moment, and even lean into the pain, it has an opportunity to be diminished.

Yet most of us are conditioned by our society to have a "wanting mind."

> Much thought has at its root a dissatisfaction with what is. Wanting is the urge for the next moment to contain what this moment does not. When there's wanting in the mind, that moment feels incomplete. Wanting is seeking elsewhere. Completeness is being right here.[3]
>
> STEPHEN LEVINE

Many of us try to get out of pain as fast as we can, so we can be more "useful" to God. Yet God reminds us again and again throughout Scripture that his greatest treasure fills earthen vessels, in order to show that the transcendent power belongs to God and not to us (II Corinthians 4:7). In our weakness, we are strong (II Corinthians 12).

Earthen vessels are God's first choice. Let God fill you just as you are. Let him touch you and use you in your fragile and fallible state.

St. Augustine said, "Lack of faith is not remembering what God has done for you in the past." Sometimes amidst pain, overwhelming grief, or undercurrents of sadness, it's difficult to remember how much God has done.

But one of the ways that our faith expresses itself is by our ability to be still, to be present, and not to panic or lose perspective. God still does his best work in the most difficult of circumstances. The Spirit is more powerful than the will, more powerful than the flesh, more powerful than pain, more powerful than guilt, even more powerful than our weakness and our doubt.

We can experience the living Christ here and now, and our difficult circumstances will be the very opportunity for our faith to grow.

## Haven't You Been Healed?

For years, people have asked me, "Haven't you prayed to the Lord for healing?"

My obvious answer: "Of course."

"Why do you think he hasn't healed you?"

"He has."

"But I thought you were still in pain."

"I am."

"I don't understand."

"I have prayed hundreds, if not thousands, of times for the Lord to heal me—and he finally *healed me of the need to be healed*." I had discovered a peace inside the pain.

I finally came to the realization that if the Lord could

use this body better the way it is, then that's the way it should be. I'm quite sure that I would be a different person, were it not for my accident. For the past ten years, I've had the opportunity to be on the steepest learning curve of my whole life. I feel like I've gotten a Ph.D. in living.

Although I could not bear the thought of having to repeat some of the experiences of the past ten years, I cannot imagine my life without them. I know that the assets have far outweighed the losses and liabilities. But still I confess, had I known what would be involved, I would probably not have had the courage to sign up for the course.

## I Shall Not Want

There is a difference between memorizing Scripture and thinking biblically. There's a difference between knowing the words and experiencing their meaning. There is a difference between having the sentences embedded in your head and having their impact embedded in your heart. There is a difference between believing that the words are right and knowing that they are true. There is a difference between "doing Christianity" and *being* a Christian.

You can memorize all of the words, but if you've forgotten the music, or never experienced it firsthand, then you still won't be able to sing the song with fullness. You'll still miss the dance. Most people say that we don't know enough Scripture. That's probably true. Paradoxically, however, we sometimes read it too much and experience it too little. Chuck Swindoll says we're called to read Scripture so deeply that our "blood runs Biblene."

Shortly after my accident, I came to the realization that I didn't know enough of Scripture to be "true truth" by *experience*. Concerned that too much of my Christian walk could get taken up with mere rhetoric, I began a curious experiment of faith. I decided to make a fifty-year commitment to understanding one verse of Scripture. The passage that I picked, or could I say that picked me, was a simple one. Memorizing it was not hard. But understanding it and experiencing it has been one of the great adventures of my life. I know more now than I did when I started, but I'm glad that I still have forty years to go. It's not just that I'm a slow learner—but that God's Word is so alive, incredibly rich and deep.

I had learned the words to Psalm 23:1 when I was a young child: "The Lord is my shepherd; I shall not want." Now I'm trying to understand the music behind the notes, the resonance beneath the surface, the substance beneath the form. Thirty-one vowels and consonants, shaped into a particular truth that, if properly understood and experienced, could reshape our lives.

I'll never forget the first day I really began to try to understand what this simple and profound sentence, so lost in familiarity, could possibly mean. I was driving a busload of college students back from a wilderness trip, and I was surprised to find myself spending the first three and a half hours meditating on the word *the*. It's a word I usually overlook, just a bookend for sentences or a filler between the real stuff like nouns and verbs. The thing that drew me was the realization that the word *the* is always used to preface a statement of reality. *The* table. *The* book. *The* person. I got so excited that I forgot to stop in the town that I was supposed to and had to turn around and come back. Quite honestly, I've not been able to look at the word *the* in the same way ever again.

Such was the beginning of my peculiar and particular journey in the understanding of Scripture at a new level. My inquiring has led me to read it, that sentence, in every version possible.

- The Lord is my shepherd; I shall not want.
- The Lord is my shepherd; therefore, I lack nothing.
- Because the Lord is my shepherd, I have everything that I need.
- The Lord is my shepherd; I shall want nothing.

Each version reminds me in a new way that the Lord is the source, the purpose, the power, the privilege of my existence.

Recently I realized that this first sentence ties together and is actually the theme of the entire psalm. For example, "The Lord is my shepherd; therefore, I shall not want for *rest* (He makes me to lie down in green pastures).

In my own life the word that I would have to keep underlining is *makes*. It seems as though the last ten years have been a process of God's constantly *making* me lie down, so that I will look up to him. Making me stop, so that I can hear his voice. As T. S. Eliot says, "In the stillness is the dancing." Each year God teaches me more and more what it means to lie down, to live out of rest. I'm learning that I have to lay down my ambitions, my dreams, my ideas.

It's only by cracking our very nature that God is able to even begin to make us vessels for his living word. We are called to be crucified with Christ.

126

When I was younger and struggling hard with that concept, I asked a saintly, elderly woman, "Why, if my old nature has been crucified with Christ, does it continue to keep on wiggling?"

She smiled and said in a quiet voice, "You must remember, Tim, that crucifixion is a *slow* death."

A. W. Tozer says there are three marks of one who is crucified. One, he is facing in only one direction. Two, he can never turn back. And three, he no longer has any plans of his own.

"The Lord is my shepherd; I shall not want." How I long for that kind of absolute surrender.

The Lord is my shepherd; I shall not want for *guidance* ("And for his name's sake, he guides me in the right path"). I was asked not too long ago what some of my options were in life. For me, it's real simple. As much as I stray, I know that my ultimate goal is simply to have him guide me on the right path for his name's sake. How do we know if it is the Lord speaking or someone else? The only answer I know is to become very familiar with his voice by spending time alone with him.

The Lord is my shepherd; I shall not want for *renewal* ("He renews life within me"). God is in the renewal business. One of the most exciting things I know about joy is that it can be restored, no matter how impossible our situation may seem. Psalm 51:12 says: "O Lord, restore me to the joy of thy salvation." Renewal is more than mere repair, more than just knocking out a few dents. It's an inside-out job. The New Testament word for it is *metanoia,* which means to be transformed or completely renewed. In Christ we are new creatures altogether, and this is a continual *process*, not merely a once-in-a-lifetime thing.

The Lord is my shepherd; I shall not want for *courage* ("Even though I walk through the valley as dark as death, I fear no evil, for thou art with me; thy staff and thy crook are my comfort"). The longer I live, the more important I believe courage is. The most important level of courage is to accept ourselves solely, when our world bombards us with messages to the contrary. The courage to love ourselves (which is a *commandment* in Scripture, and not merely a "suggestion") in the midst of all the turmoil and confusion and urgency which pushes and pulls at us each day. And then, the courage to forget ourselves in recklessly loving a hurting world with the genuine love of Christ.

The Lord is my shepherd; I shall not want for *joy* ("Thou spreadest a table before me in the sight of my enemies. Thou hast richly bathed my head with oil and my cup runs over"). In the Old Testament, oil almost always represents gladness or joy. It was an essential part of many spiritual celebrations. Joy is one of the surest signs of the presence of God, and the promise here is to be bathed in oil to such an extent that our cup runs over.

The Lord is my shepherd; I shall not want for *mercy.* It has been said that grace is getting what we don't deserve, and mercy is *not* getting what we *do* deserve. When I was younger, mercy was a rather distant word to me. These days it's a very tangible reality. I know myself well enough to realize how much I have fouled up my life and am in need of God's mercy.

The Lord is my shepherd; therefore, I shall not want *forever* ("And I will dwell in the house of the Lord forever," v. 6). Eternity is a rather long time. Most of our minds are incapable of even starting to comprehend what it means. I don't think about eternity a lot.

But when I do, I'm grateful to know that it's in his hands and not mine, and that I shall not be found wanting. Eternal life began when the first connection and commitment was made to Jesus Christ. According to the rumor, it has no end. I rather like that.

These are only a few thoughts from a marvelous time of learning. I look forward to the next forty years of discovery. One of the insights on Psalm 23:1 comes from a beautiful book, *I Shall Not Want*, by Robert Ketchum (to whom I owe many of the previous insights as well). He tells of a Sunday school teacher who asked her group of children if anyone could quote the entire twenty-third psalm. A golden-haired four-and-a-half-year-old girl was among those who raised their hands. A bit skeptical, the teacher asked if she could really quote the entire psalm. The little girl came to the rostrum, faced the class, made a perky little bow, and said: "The Lord is my shepherd, *that's all I want.*" She bowed again and went and sat down. That may well be the greatest interpretation I've ever heard. And it is a beautiful reminder to me of who I want to become.

# Muffled Triumph

*He is the Way. Follow Him through the Land of Unlikeness;
You will see rare beasts, and have unique adventures.*

*He is the Truth. Seek Him in the Kingdom of Anxiety; You
will come to a great city that has expected your return for years.*

*He is the Life. Love Him in the World of the Flesh; And at
your marriage all of its occasions shall dance for joy.[1]*

W. H. AUDEN

*As for me, I've tasted a little from every cup and grown
through the struggles. I have loved until I ached from loving,
and wept until my heart was sick of tears. I have known life in
all its complexity—and looking back, I would not undo one
moment, if I could.[2]*

MARILEE ZDENEK

I'VE NOTICED, ESPECIALLY IN THE PAST FEW YEARS, that I
tend to avoid books with the word *victorious* in the title.
Somehow they don't seem to speak to where I am. My
journey just isn't described in such simple terms. I've
struggled with the fact that I am unambiguously Christian and at the same time, unmistakably human. In fact,

131

my journey has become more human, not less, since I encountered this one called Christ.

And the journey continues; the process isn't over yet. I still have many opportunities to laugh, love, and learn in new ways.

\* \* \*

*Spring, 1985*
*I feel like I've got a headache all over my body, and I'm still nauseated. Who knows . . . maybe I'm pregnant.*

*Pain again. Or should I say still. I haven't slept through a whole night for almost nine weeks. After ten years, I'm weary of it. Every inch of me wants a break. I feel like a butterfly that is still alive, but pinned wiggling to a board. Aspirin, pain pills, prayer. More prayer, more aspirin, more pain pills. Sometimes nothing seems to work.*

*You are enough. "This priceless treasure we hold, so to speak, in common earthenware—to show that the splendid power of it belongs to God and not to us. . . . We are puzzled, but never in despair. . . . We may be knocked down but we are never knocked out! Every day we experience something of the death of Jesus, so that we may also show the power of the life of Jesus in these bodies of ours" (II Corinthians 4:7-10, Phillips). You are enough! I just need a little more "wait training." In the midst of all this, your joy grows deeper still.*

\* \* \*

I've survived because I've discovered a new and different kind of joy that I never knew existed—a joy that can coexist with uncertainty and doubt, pain, confusion, and ambiguity. A journal entry a couple of years ago, written in the midst of the most trying period

132

I've ever experienced, says simply "I gave up looking for certainty—and found truth." I realized that when I quit waiting for certainty to come, I was free to discover, or rediscover, the essence of what I was really looking for.

Joy is a process, a journey—often muffled, sometimes detoured; a mystery in which we participate, not a product we can grasp. It grows and regenerates as we have the courage to let go and trust the process. Growth and joy are inhibited when we say "if only," enhanced when we realize that failures and difficulties are not only a critical part of the process, but are our very opportunities to grow.

When we give up our excessive need for security and "clean victories," for everything to be right, then the peace that passes all understanding has room to invade our lives again.

Dr. Frank Carver is one of the most dedicated and brilliant men I know. As chairman of the Department of Religion at Point Loma Nazarene College, he has obviously studied the Christian faith over decades of discipline.

We had the privilege of having Dr. Carver on one of our Summit Expedition Wilderness courses for adults. His snow-white hair and beard added to his look of wisdom. Throughout the week his insights during times of dialogue stunned us.

One moment, when just he and I were talking, he said something I'll never forget:

> In recent years, I've learned three things that have changed how I view my life in a considerable way. The first is that my primary opportunity and obligation in life is to be a Christian—not a department head, not a pastor, not any of the many roles I play.

The second thing is that I don't know what that actually means. I am called, as Paul says, to be a steward of the mystery of Christ.

And third, because of this I am forced to my knees each day to discover by grace what it means and how I live it out.

His words had a profound impact on me. I was moved that a man of his stature, who has taught religion for so many years, would be so open, honest, and humble. But even more than that, it gave me confidence to let go in some new ways—to realize again that we trust a Person, not a set of answers. And this Person is often, if not always, different from who we think he is.

Robert M. Brown begins a chapter of his *The Bible Speaks to You* with a scroll on which are written the following words:

> BE IT HEREBY ENACTED:
> That every three years all people
> Shall forget whatever they have learned
> About Jesus,
> And begin the study all over again.

While one great tragedy of the world is that many people are unfamiliar with Jesus, it is equally tragic that some of us are too familiar with him, in the sense that "we think we know, we think we really understand" the full significance of his life within us and among us.

About a year after I wrote my first book I received a letter from a former student.

Dec. 12, 1980

Dear Tim,

I've just finished reading an interesting little book

called *When I Relax I Feel Guilty.* It's not bad for a former gym teacher. What amazes me, though, is I'm still learning and being encouraged by that same gym teacher, ten years after I graduated from Menlo-Atherton High.

I may not be burned deeply into your memory, Tim, but you are in mine. And now that you've surfaced once again in my life, I thought I'd let you know that.

I remember the first day I had you for P.E. when I was a freshman in 1966. We all had to run the 600-yard dash and I didn't want to. I was always coming in last, no matter how hard I ran (and I always ran as hard as I could). But this one was different.

Oh, I still came in last—by about 150 yards, as I remember. But I remember you running along side of me that last 100 yards yelling, "Good effort, Lou! Great effort! Absolutely magnificent. . . ."

I felt like I'd won the Olympic Gold Medal for the marathon. And I became totally devoted to you because no one had ever encouraged me like you.

The next year I was your manager for the soccer team, a position I took [again the following year]—despite the fact that you had left to circumnavigate the globe—but left the next year to play fullback for the JVs—when you returned.

And I would never had the courage to do it, if it had not been for your example.

Well, that was more than a decade ago. I went to college and majored in journalism because my senior English teacher told me I had no ability as a writer (I never liked him much and I had become fascinated by things I supposedly could not do). All through those four years I held your example in my mind, looked for possibilities and wondered—often—how you always managed to be so positive all the time.

Five years ago I met Jesus and figured you out.


To me, one of the most exciting things about the Christian faith is that we'll never fully understand it.

One of the most attractive things about Jesus is that we can't fully comprehend him. And one of the most important things I know about the joy he wants to give us is that it's different from what we think it is.

Ours is an age that wants to neatly wrap everything in cellophane. We want answers, not process. We're trained to come to conclusions which, when captured, we can control. The only problem is that it doesn't work in every area of our lives.

> He who binds to himself a joy
> Does the winged life destroy;
> But he who kisses the joy as it flies
> Lives in eternity's sunrise.
> WILLIAM BLAKE

I think two of the reasons why most people miss joy are (1) they have preconceived images of what joy is supposed to be, and (2) they try to cling to those experiences, to keep and preserve them.

Perhaps one of the best things I've been forced to learn over the past ten years is to let go of my preconceived images about God, about life, about others, and about myself. I've discovered that I am less—and more—than what I had imagined: both more whole and more fragmented, stronger and more fragile, more selfish and more capable of genuine love.

At least for me, it is less the *victorious* Christian life than the *notorious* Christian life, because for me it is constantly new, changing, different, and far more powerful than anything I'd dreamed it to be.

I think of Howard Butt's profoundly simple question: "Which would you rather have—a Christian reputation or Jesus Christ?" and know again that it is not vital for me to appear to others to be a "victorious

136

Christian." If this process has taught me anything, it is to be who I am in Christ, without images or pretense. I am slowly learning what it means to be free in Christ.

Being justified in Christ means, among other things, that I don't have to keep continually justifying myself. I am slowly discovering a radical (in the sense of its etymology, "rooted") kind of self-acceptance—because of and in spite of my limitations.

Truth is free, but not easy. I began to be set free to live—to reinhabit my true self, warts and all. As I let go of my rigid expectations and self-importance, I discovered a new kind of triumph that didn't have to look victorious. One evening I sat down and described it in a poem, "Muffled Triumph."

Mine is only a muffled triumph,
  Joy mingled with still-ever-constant pain
    an unjustifiable gladness
      of merely being alive.

The daily confrontations often leave me
  Less than the best
    But still
Something ever new keeps emerging
  Hope—now deeper, more enduring
Love—yes, but in unsentimental dailyness
Faith—not enough to move mountains
  But just enough to keep me
    in muffled triumph.

# With Gladness and Hunger

*Be patient toward all that is unsolved in your heart and try to love the questions themselves, like locked rooms and like books that are now written in a very foreign tongue. Do not now seek the answers, which cannot be given you because you would not be able to live them. And the point is, to live everything. Live the questions now. Perhaps you will then gradually, without noticing it, live along some distant day into the answer.* [1]

MARIA RANIER RILKE

*O God, enlarge my horizons.*

I CHRONICLES 4:10

*There are no rules for leaping into the new, because no one has ever been there before.*

SISTER CORITA

IT WAS THE MIDDLE OF WORLD WAR II. Men were giving their best on the front lines. Somehow one of them scrounged up an old beaten-up phonograph and a record. The record was of none other than Enrico Caruso, considered at that time the greatest singer in the world.

139

That evening as they sat around the tent listening to the scratchy, rather worn record on a weathered phonograph, there were two distinct groups of listeners. Some heard only the scratches on the record. Others, who listened more deeply, heard the master's voice.

My hope is that somehow, by God's grace, you've been able to read and hear beyond the scratches in my record to "hear the Master's voice."

It's difficult to know how to close a book like this. Because in many ways, certainly for me and I hope as well for you, this is not the conclusion, but the beginning. It's been a long journey, a special journey. And I suspect, because of this one they call Jesus, it's not only far from over, but the best is yet to come.

I've learned more than I can put on pages. My prayer is that you've learned more than you read here in black and white. I've long since learned, in both writing and speaking, that it's not what I say that counts, but what people hear and understand. And God is the only true teacher. But yet, I am aware of the power of words.

> [This teacher] was the first to give me a feeling for what words are, and can do, in themselves. Through him I started to sense that words not only convey something, but *are* something; that words have color, depth, texture of their own, and power to evoke vastly more than they mean; that words can be used not merely to make things clear, make things vivid, make things interesting and whatever else, but to make things happen inside the one who reads them or hears them. [2]
>
> FREDERICK BUECHNER

I got a second chance at life. That's basically what this book has been all about—a second chance for you as well to discover not only the immense privilege of living, but also all of life's delicious pieces. Each day continues to give me a new opportunity to learn, to love and laugh, learn and grow, fail and get up again, struggle and lose, persevere and get to know our Lord in a more personal and intense way.

This journey, which I believe is sacred, almost cost me my life and my family. One night I was speaking about the genuine, concrete, tangible, unextinguishable joy I've discovered in the process and a man came up to me afterwards and said, "You almost make me want to fall into a crevasse so I can discover how special life really is."

I don't recommend this particular process. Each of us gets a second chance every day, if we would just open our eyes to the possibilities. Each of us is his or her own story. May each of us continue to allow God to write his unique and indelible story in each of our lives.

There will be more questions than answers, but the living out of those questions, honestly and joyfully, may be the most genuine and realistic response to our life of faith.

We all long for certainty and security, the fulfillment of our many questions, but the life of faith implies living the questions, wandering through our fears and hopes, and somehow shuffling our way with tenacity and courage toward Bethlehem. Robert Raines says that "The Bible is a book of journeys and questions—of people asking God questions and God questioning his people."

The point now is to live the questions out as fully as possible with gladness and hunger. The most important thing to keep remembering is that life is not so much meant to be understood as it is to be lived out; it is not a problem to be solved, but a mystery to be participated in fully. Let yourself be surprised.

> To believe in God is to know
> That all the rules will be fair—
> And that there will be many surprises!
>
> SISTER CORITA

When I became a Christian at Stanford, I had strong, neat, crisp images of what my future was going to be like. I was going to be physically strong, for Christ's sake. I was going to be intellectually acute (B.A., M.A. from Stanford). I was going to be emotionally bomb-proof—and spiritually profound. I wanted and intended to be the very best that I could be—to honor the Kingdom. But as you have seen, it didn't quite turn out that way. My life, my story, turned out differently than my original script.

> We may desire to bring to the Lord a perfect work. We would like to point, when our work is done, to the beautiful ripened grain, and bound-up sheaves, and yet the Lord frustrates our plans, shatters our purposes, lets us see the wreck of all our hopes, breaks the beautiful structure we thought we were building and catches us up in his arms and whispers to us, "It's not your work I wanted, but you."
>
> SOURCE UNKNOWN

In the Book of Job it says that God will test us and try us until we "come forth as gold" (Job 23:10). Someone once asked a goldsmith how long he kept the gold in the fire. His reply: "Until I can see my face in it."

In his marvelous and mysterious way, God keeps shaping us until he can see himself in our lives. The process is long, arduous, complex, and certainly not painless, but it's worth it. And we need not wait until the conclusion to celebrate. We can, if we choose, genuinely celebrate the process.

*There is no box
  made by God
  nor us
but that the sides can be flattened out
  and the top blown off
  to make a dance floor
  on which to celebrate life.*

KENNETH CARAWAY

# Notes

## AN ETERNAL MOMENT IN TIME

1. Annie Dillard, *Pilgrim at Tinker Creek* (New York: Harper & Row, 1974), p. 90.

## BREAKDOWN OR BREAKTHROUGH

1. Clyde Reid, *Celebrate the Temporary* (New York: Harper & Row, 1972), pp. 43, 44, 45.

## CHOOSE JOY

1. Lewis B. Smedes, *How Can It Be All Right When Everything Is All Wrong* (New York: Harper & Row, 1982), pp. 11, 15.

2. John Shea, "The Storyteller of God," quoted in *Lord of the Dance* by Andrew M. Greeley (New York: Warner Books, 1984).

3. G. W. Target, "The Window" from *The Window and Other Essays* (Mountain View, California: Pacific Press Publishing Association, 1973), pp. 5-7. Used by permission.

4. Erich Fromm, *To Have or to Be?* (New York: Bantam Books, 1976), p. 10.

5. Taken from *Traveling Light* by Eugene H. Peterson. © 1982 by Inter-Varsity Christian Fellowship of the United States of America and used by permission of InterVarsity Press, Downers Grove, IL.

## BITE THE BULLET

1. Norman Cousins, *Anatomy of an Illness as Perceived by the Patient* (New York: W. W. Norton & Co., 1979), p. 86.

2. Merle Shain, *When Lovers Are Friends* (New York: Bantam Books, 1978), p. 65.

## MERE LIFE

1. Sydney Carter, © 1963 Galliard Ltd. Used by permission of Galaxy Music Corporation, NY. Sole U.S. agent. All rights reserved.

2. Sister Corita, quoted by Joseph Pintauro in *To Believe in Man* (New York: Harper & Row, 1970).

3. Excerpted from page 51 of *Wishful Thinking: A Theological ABC* by Frederick Buechner. © 1973 by Frederick Buechner. Reprinted by permission of Harper & Row Publishers, Inc.

4. Gerhard E. Frost, *Blessed Is the Ordinary* (Minneapolis: Winston Press, 1980).

5. Excerpted from "Don't Miss the Miracle" in *Three Days to See* by Helen Keller. First published in *Atlantic Monthly*, 1933. © American Foundation for the Blind. Used by permission.

6. Richard L. Evans, "What Are We Waiting For?" quoted by Mark Link, S.J., in *In the Stillness Is the Dancing* (Niles, IL: Argus Communications, 1972), p. 11.

7. From the poem "stand with your lover on the ending earth—" © 1949 by E. E. Cummings, reprinted from his volume *Complete Poems—1913-1962* by permission of Harcourt Brace Jonanovich, Inc., New York.

8. Scott Peck, *The Road Less Traveled* (New York: Simon & Schuster, 1978), p. 15.

9. Eugene Kennedy, *Living with Everyday Problems* (Chicago: Thomas More Press, 1974), pp. 10, 13.

10. These examples were taken from a quotation by MacDonald in *Leaves of Gold* © 1948 by A. C. and D. G. Remley (The Coslett Publishing Co., Williamsport, PA).

## THE ADVANTAGES OF DISADVANTAGES

1. The story "Sarge" by Mary Moore appeared in the January, 1965, issue of *Reader's Digest* (Pleasantville, NY 10570).

2. Anthony Pabovano, *The Human Journey* (Garden City, NY: Doubleday, 1982).

3. From *God Is No Fool* by Lois Cheney. © 1969 by Abingdon Press (Nashville, TN). Used by permission.

4. Frederick Buechner, *The Sacred Journey* (San Francisco: Harper & Row, 1982), p. 46.


## PEACE INSIDE THE PAIN

1. William Stafford as quoted by Eugene H. Peterson in *Run with the Horses* (Downers Grove, IL: InterVarsity Press, 1983), p. 30.

2. Eugene Kennedy, *The Pain of Being Human* (Garden City, NY: Image Books, 1972), introduction.

3. Stephen Levine, *A Gradual Awakening* (Garden City, NY: Anchor Books, 1979), p. 13.


## MUFFLED TRIUMPH

1. W. H. Auden, from the poem "For the Time Being" in *Collected Poems* (New York: Random House, 1976), p. 308.

2. Marilee Zdenek, *Splinters in My Pride* (Waco, TX: Word, Inc. 1979).


## WITH GLADNESS AND HUNGER

1. Rainer M. Rilke, *Letters to a Young Poet* (New York: W. W. Norton & Co., Inc., revised edition 1963), p. 35.

2. Frederick Buechner, *The Sacred Journey* (San Francisco: Harper & Row, 1982), p. 68.

# Dancin' Shoes

The phone call was from home. "They're taking Dad into the hospital again. Maybe for the last time."

His long battle with cancer was nearly over.

"How's he taking it, Mom?"

"Oh, you know him. He's still chipper. I'll give you a call tonight to let you know how he's doing. And if something happens, you know as well as I do how incredibly blessed we've been. He's already fooled the doctors for over three years."

I knew it well. The year before we had all prayed that Dad would live long enough to see my *What Kids Need Most in a Dad* come out, since it was in a very real way a tribute to him. I was hoping he would be able to see this book, too, but it seemed he had an earlier deadline to meet than I did.

I hung up the phone and thought about a line from a poem I'd read recently—"God himself is fitting you with a whole new pair of dancing shoes." And I sat down and wrote a few lines to my dad.

*Get your dancin' shoes ready, Pop. That's what you and Mom have always been good at, no matter what the circum-*

149

*stances. You gotta keep dancin', Pop. I'm counting on you.*

At five-fifty a.m. on May 2, 1985, Art Hansel put on his new dancin' shoes, just one week before this book was finished. My mom, my brother Steve, and I were all there for the final family reunion, and were all with my father when he passed away.

He died the same way he lived, quietly and gracefully. He was a magnificent person, and though a man of few words, he echoed with his entire life what this book has been trying to say.

*Hey . . . I love you, Pop! And I'm gonna miss you, too.*

*Keep those dancin' shoes handy, because when I come I'm bringing mine, too—and we'll celebrate all that God has done for us.*

*See ya soon, Pop.*

*Tim*

Tim Hansel is president of Summit Expedition, a nonprofit California corporation providing adventure-based educational experiences for people of all ages and backgrounds. Tim is also highly sought after as a speaker and seminar leader. For more information about Summit Expedition, or for information regarding films, books, or speaking engagements, write to:

Tim Hansel
Summit Expedition
P.O. Box 521
San Dimas, California 91773

or call 818/915-3331


For copies of *When I Relax I Feel Guilty,* Tim Hansel's down-to-earth book about the hows and whys of a relaxed, joyous, and godly life-style, contact your local Christian bookstore or write:

David C. Cook Publishing Co.
850 N. Grove
Elgin, Illinois 60120